The
Perfect
Life

The Perfect Life

TEN PRINCIPLES
AND PRACTICES TO
TRANSFORM YOUR LIFE

Marc Allen

NEW WORLD LIBRARY
SAN RAFAEL · CALIFORNIA

© 1992 Marc Allen

Published by New World Library
58 Paul Drive
San Rafael, CA 94903

Cover design: Kathleen Vande Kieft
Text design: Stephanie Young
Composition: Harrington-Young Typography
Albany, California

Library of Congress Cataloging-in-Publication Data

Allen, Mark, 1946–   The perfect life / Marc Allen.
      p.   cm.
    Includes bibliographic references and index.
    ISBN 0-931432-85-5
    1. Success—Psychological aspects.   I. Title.
BF637.S8A397   1992
158'.1—dc 20   91-40642
                                        CIP

First printing, February 1992
Printed in the U.S.A. on acid-free paper
ISBN 0-931432-85-5

.

This book is dedicated
to you

.

·

Human life by its very nature is filled with vulnerabilities, trial and error, and learning. Expecting ourselves to behave in some perfect way or to attain perfect results is not realistic.

We need to shift the focus from trying to attain perfect results or to live up to perfect standards to recognizing the innate perfection in the process or in the journey. The life force has an incredible perfection about it. As we're learning to recognize and follow the life force, we will see the perfection of the process, how everything we need to learn is brought to us in some amazing way that we could never have figured out or understood.

Shakti Gawain
—<u>Awakening</u>

Contents

————————— • —————————

To live your life
    in your own way
To reach the goals
    you've set for yourself
To be the person
    you want to be —
    that is success

(Author unknown)

Acknowledgments

———————— • ————————

I'd like to thank my parents, William and Anne Donicht, for their unwavering love and support. They are living proof that you can still be deeply in love after over fifty years of marriage.

Deep thanks as well to Shakti Gawain. Knowing her has changed the course of my life.

Thanks to everyone at New World Library for their support and assistance. Thanks especially to Janet Mills for her insight, and for a great deal of work above and beyond the call of duty. Thanks to Carol LaRusso and Marianne Rogoff for their excellent help in editing.

Introduction:
The Perfect Life

———————— • ————————

*Since everything is but an apparition,
perfect in being what it is, having nothing
to do with good or bad or right or wrong,
one might as well burst out in laughter.*

—Long Chen Pa
Tibet, ca. 1300

Is it really possible to have a perfect life?

It is—if we understand that the perfect life does not involve striving to attain some impossible ideal of perfection, or realizing a fleeting fantasy of how we might ideally live.

Creating the perfect life means understanding that the *process* of our lives—the ongoing growth and development we all experience as we grow older—is in itself totally perfect.

Every moment of our lives has its own perfect reason for being, its own absolute perfection. And, once we understand how, we can use each moment of our lives to create the life we want—the perfect life.

It happens to be Thanksgiving Day as I write these words. The hills outside my window are bathed in the sparkling light of a warm, clear morning. I certainly have a lot to be thankful for—as most of us do, when we think about it. I have my health, my family and friends, my emotional well-being, my material wealth; I have my desire to create things of value, and the means to make these available to the world. I have the feeling that my life has meaning, and that my work has made a positive contribution in the world.

Perhaps the greatest thing I have to be thankful for is the knowledge I have gained, along the way—knowledge that can be communicated to others. The essence of this knowledge can be summed up in a few simple statements; while the words are simple, realizing and living the words is difficult—and the greatest, most worthwhile challenge there is. These words summarize this entire book:

Your success in the world, your ability to create the kind of life you want, does not rely on your talent or ability or intelligence or luck or environment or education or family. *Your ability to create the life you want lies solely in your willingness to clearly conceive of what you want, to create realistic goals to get there, to keep moving toward those goals, and to emotionally prepare for your success by confronting the doubts, fears, and problems that prevent you from creating the life you want.*

Your success in life, or your lack of success, is completely up to you.

If you can understand this, not only with your head, but with your heart, and if you can put it into action, you will be successful in creating the perfect life. It is inevitable. It is up to you.

1
A Beginning

———— • ————

*You will become as great as your
dominant aspiration. . . . If you cherish a
vision, a lofty ideal in your heart, you will
realize it.*

—James Allen
<u>As You Think</u>

I'll begin by briefly telling how I discovered the principles and techniques that have shown me how to create the life I want, the life I dare to call the perfect life.

The most important turning point in my life came on the day of my thirtieth birthday. I spent most of the day alone, pacing back and forth in my little studio apartment in Oakland, California —a place I can only describe as a slum apartment. I spent hours reflecting upon my life, and I began to see it in a new light, and from a broader perspective.

Unlike so many people I had known, I had always done what I wanted to do in my life. I had never made the mistake, in my opinion, of putting aside the things I was excited and passionate about and choosing instead to do things that seemed safer or more reasonable, or that seemed to provide more security. I had spent most of my early years in a passionate love affair with theater and music, becoming a professional actor and musician when I was a teenager. After college I became involved in spiritual pursuits, especially yoga and Zen and Tibetan Buddhism, and I spent six years studying them, attempting to adapt them to Western culture as well as to my own life.

But it wasn't until I turned thirty that I realized it was time to do some serious thinking about my life: past, present, and future. It became painfully clear to me that all through my life, I had never really made any kind of definite plan that I could follow. I wasn't directing the play of my life, I was just acting it out, doing things other, stronger individuals led me into—even though I always went willingly, excited by each new challenge.

The whole pattern suddenly became clear to me: I had been a follower, drifting all of my life instead of determining my own destiny, and now I had nothing to show—at least materially—for thirty years of growth and study and work. I had no money, no assets, except for some musical equipment of steadily depreciating value. I didn't even own a car. I had gained something very valuable emotionally, and spiritually, from my years of meditation. I had gained a degree of calmness, even serenity at times, and an awareness of an intuitive voice within, a quiet masterful voice I was learning to identify and listen to. But it was not enough; I was unsatisfied with so many things in my life. I felt as if I was drifting, completely without direction. And my serenity couldn't pay the rent.

It was time to take control of my life, to ask myself some important questions: What do I really want to do with my life? What am I here for? It was time to get motivated, to discover my potential, and to take some steps toward realizing that potential.

It was frightening, and challenging, yet I knew that my life had to change. And I knew it was up to me to change it—no one else could do it for me.

THE IDEAL SCENE

I asked my intuitive mind where to begin, something I do often: I simply ask myself a question, and pause, relax, and wait for an answer to appear. I know the answer comes from my intuitive mind when there is a feeling of truth, of calmness, of *rightness* to it. I always get an answer, even though the answer has sometimes been, "You're not ready for the answer yet—wait awhile." Or, "That's not the right question to ask at this time."

I asked myself where to begin to start steering my life in some kind of direction. My intuition said, "Remember that 'ideal scene' game you once played? Start there."

This is a game in which you assume five years has passed, and everything has happened as perfectly, as ideally, as you can possibly imagine. What would your life look like? What would you be doing?

What if five years had passed, and I was living the perfect life—what would it look like? It didn't take long at all for a picture to form: I owned my own home, in a peaceful, quiet part of beautiful Marin County, north of San Francisco. The house was white, filled with light, with a swimming pool, and I was paying for it effortlessly, with no struggle at all. I was writing a steady stream of books that sold well, and contributed, each in its own way, to a better world. I was creating successful albums, filled with beautiful music that people loved. And I had built a successful book publishing and record company to serve as a vehicle for my books and music. I didn't want to be in the powerless position of writers or artists who have to keep searching for a company to release their work. The company ran smoothly, like a well-oiled machine, and was highly profitable. It was a successful model of a thriving business serving to inspire the world. I had created it all without excessive struggle or stress, without becoming a workaholic; I had plenty of spare time to do as I wished, being as relaxed—even as lazy—as I wanted to be.

The scene that sprang to mind was far removed from my then-current reality—living below the poverty line in a noisy slum apartment. I had not yet written a book—though I had dreams of doing so, and a few piles of notes here and there. I had released an album, but not of my own music, and not on my own label. I didn't have a publishing company. I didn't have any family members or friends who were able to invest in my dreams. I knew nothing about business.

I had a lot to learn, but I had stumbled upon something important. Although I didn't know it at the time, this game I played—creating an ideal scene—would become the first major step in creating the life I wanted.

Looking at that ideal scene felt so good and so satisfying, so significant and so expansive. I realized that something very valuable was hidden within that ideal scene: my purpose, or mission, in life. I was able to express this purpose in a single, simple sentence. Later on, I'll ask you to imagine your own ideal scene, and to reflect upon and express your purpose or mission in life.

LONG-TERM GOALS

That ideal scene contained several long-term goals that I could easily break down into a number of short-term goals. These centered around writing books, producing music, and establishing a publishing and record company. As soon as I reflected on all of this, an inner voice cried out, loud and clear, "No! It's too much! Books *and* music, art *and* business. Pick one or the other—the books, or the music, and focus on just one of these."

Was this voice intuition, or just doubt and fear? From the quality of the voice, and from the agitation that I felt, I knew it was the voice of fear speaking—fear of expansion, fear of expressing myself, fear of spreading myself too thin, fear of ridicule, fear of failure, perhaps even fear of success. It was not my intuition. My intuition quietly hummed along, as usual; I asked myself, "Should I pick just one or the other, books or music?" And my intuitive voice simply replied, "No, do them both, do it all. You can have it all. There are two very different sides of yourself that need to be expressed, and each is a good balance for the other. Besides, one will undoubtedly become more successful than the other, and will help support the other—but you won't know which will do which, until you do them both."

It was a challenge: writing books *and* music, creating a business as well as art. But the challenge felt exciting, and I sensed that it was in alignment with my greatest purpose in life. I felt that, in some way, it was what I had come here to do.

When I reflected upon my ideal scene, four long-term goals immediately sprang to mind: (1) Write my first book; (2) record my first album; (3) publish my first book; (4) release my first album. Then I realized that before I could start any of these, I would need some money. And so my first short-term goal sprang to mind: *Get a job, any kind of job, and make some money.* It seems so obvious, even comical, now—but it wasn't at the time. I hadn't been focused on any kind of long-range goals, and I saw no need to work in a job that I didn't particularly like. But now my attitude changed: I decided to work at any kind of job, and try to save at least *twenty percent* to invest in my book and record projects.

THE PLAN

Without being consciously aware of it, I had created a simple, workable business plan: I would work in any kind of job I could get for as long as necessary, and save a portion of my income to invest in my projects. Eventually I would create my own publishing and record company, and produce my books and music myself.

I didn't have many skills I could use to get a job, but I did have a basic understanding of how to typeset books. I looked under "Typesetting" in the yellow pages, and got a job within a week.

THE FIRST PROJECTS

I realized my ideal scene and long-term goals didn't come out of nowhere, for I had been working toward them, subconsciously, for some time. During the next six months or so, I transformed one of my piles of notes I had collected into something that technically could be called a book, though it was crudely produced. I printed three hundred copies, and realized I had achieved two of my first four goals: I had written a book and published a book.

Before too long, a friend and I completed a simple album on a little four-track home studio, and I managed to save twelve hundred dollars to print a thousand copies of our first album, titled "Breathe." Within a year or so all four goals had been reached; then the challenge—the next series of goals—became not only to create a publishing company and a record company, but to create a *successful* company as well. This goal took much longer to reach—seven or eight years. But, step by step, one goal at a time, we moved toward the creation of a profitable business.

TOWARD THE IDEAL SCENE

After two years of typesetting, often working fifty hours or more a week, and trying to build my little business and write my books and music on the side, I found myself close to being burned out. Something had to give; it was time for a change.

I had discovered a way of doing high-quality typesetting in my own home that didn't require very expensive equipment, and I decided, after quite a bit of trepidation, to quit my job and go into the typesetting business for myself. I set up my own little business—typing in the walk-in closet of my studio apartment—and very soon was making twenty dollars or more an hour, instead of five. I didn't work as many hours, but made more money. Only a few months after I started, it felt like all my fears had been completely unfounded.

I found I was good at typesetting, and able to teach others how to do it, so I entertained the idea of renting office space and getting several people to work for me. But something didn't feel right about it. As I thought it over, I realized it was not in alignment with my ideal scene. I wanted to write books and music and have a company as a vehicle for my writing—it was not a part of my ideal scene to be running a typesetting shop.

I had stumbled on a principle that has proven very powerful for me over the years: *By doing things that are in alignment with your ideal scene and your purpose in life, your chances of true success are greatly magnified.* In fact, they're guaranteed, unless you undermine your success through fears or addictive behavior or lack of focus or other problems, which we'll discuss later.

Within a few years, I was doing well enough to be able to move to Marin County, fulfilling another part of my ideal scene. A few years after that I was able to buy a small starter house, with a modest down payment. Slowly, step by step, I was moving toward actually living what had been a fantasy only a few years before.

Eight years later, the house had nearly doubled in value, giving me a sizable amount of equity that allowed me to move up into a beautiful light-filled home with a dream-sized swimming pool in a quiet neighborhood.

AN EMOTIONAL BREAKTHROUGH

When I bought my first house, I could see I was making progress, but there were still major pieces missing from the creation of my ideal scene. I was creating a steady stream of books and music, but they weren't selling very well. I had been able to buy a small house, but it was still a struggle, month after month, to cover all my expenses. An important part of my ideal scene, from the very beginning, had been that I wanted to be able to cover my expenses, both personal and in the business, *easily and effort-lessly.* I did not want money—or more precisely, lack of money—to be something I would struggle with all my life.

One gray winter day, as I was driving to work, I realized I was anxious, irritated, uptight. I turned off the radio and did a simplified version of the 'core belief process'—something we will explore in depth in Chapter Three. I started talking to myself—out loud in my car, as I sometimes do. I asked myself what I was so uptight about, and I answered immediately, vehemently: "*Money!* I don't like this constant shortage of money in my life; it's draining; it's no fun at all!"

I let myself babble on about my feelings, saying everything that came to mind—and in doing so explored those feelings in more depth. (It's a great form of therapy—without the expense of a therapist.) I surprised myself by saying that I felt resentful toward my father because he hadn't been able to support me in my business or my writing. I felt irritated, even angry, with him— ideally, in a perfect world, I wanted to be able to call him up and say, "Gee, Dad, cash flow's a little tight right now—I could sure use ten thousand dollars or so."

As I drove down the freeway that day, I became aware of the huge amount of frustration I had felt over the years around the issue of money. So much time had been spent, and so much energy, worrying about it, scrambling for it, doing a great deal of work for what was often very little income. I was not managing myself well financially—personally or in business.

I sat and listened to my critical voices, my frustrated voices, my childlike voices wanting a rich daddy to take care of them. Then another voice appeared, a much calmer voice, clearer and wiser— the voice of my intuition. I was surprised at what the voice said, because of its almost religious imagery. Our intuition is a subtle and delicate thing; its workings are often mysterious; its words are often surprising.

A quiet, calm inner voice said to me, "What are you getting so agitated about? Why are you blaming your father? What good will that do? There's no reason to blame him at all. Your problems with money are things *you* have created, simply because you don't understand that you *do* have a rich father, an absolutely abundant father, who can give you whatever you want in life. But it is not your physical father; it is a far greater father, your spiritual father. Just ask *him* for what you want, and he will give it to you."

I was startled; I had this image of an abundant, cosmic father, able to grant my wishes. I cried out, "Father! Please give me ten thousand dollars! I need it to relieve this financial anxiety! Tell me what to do." And I imagined myself holding a check for ten thousand dollars, made out to me.

I felt an expansive change in my mind, almost immediately, and I continued to feel it over the next several weeks. I had never before even dared to imagine how I could create or receive *ten thousand dollars*, all at one time, but now my mind was entertaining all kinds of creative ideas, usually as I was driving down the freeway on the way to or from my office. I had a feeling I was being guided, or led, to it. Perhaps I could sell a book idea to a larger publisher, for an advance. I considered several possibilities, but none of them took wing or had any life to them—probably because another part of me wanted to publish my books myself.

I came up with some ideas for mail order projects. I tried a couple of different things, including a booklet whose title is too embarrassing to repeat. They didn't work—and they cost me a few hundred dollars to advertise—but at least I was trying.

Soon after that someone called to ask for my assistance in publishing a book that he and his companion had written together. As we worked together over the next few months, he became familiar with my publishing company, and told me one day he had about ten thousand dollars he wanted to invest in some kind of enterprise. That number certainly rang a bell. I sold him a portion of my stock in the company, and he wrote me a check. I stared at that check for ten thousand dollars and knew my father had come through.

MAKING A 'PERSONAL POWER KIT'

Not long after, a friend told me about a seminar he had attended. The essence of what was taught was so simple I started doing it right away—and the results were nothing short of phenomenal:

On a single sheet of paper, list all of your long-term goals, and at the top of the page, write, *"In an easy and relaxed manner, in a healthy and positive way, in its own perfect time. . . ."* Then, for at least twenty-one days (the approximate number of days it usually takes to form a habit), read this list of goals out loud, preceding each one with that phrase.

This simple exercise had a powerful effect on the course of my life.

Once I started listing my goals, revising them occasionally to keep them current, I put my goals and the pages of my journal together in a folder, with pockets. I bought a separate notebook with a calendar in it to carry with me through the day, in which I wrote short-term goals and scheduled how to achieve them. I started thinking of the folder and the notebook as my 'personal power kit'—something we'll get into in depth later, and something that I recommend for everyone.

SUMMARY

As I look back, I can see that I have been led by my own intuition and by the guidance of others into discovering several important principles and practices. These principles have transformed my life from one of poverty to one of success—and *success is whatever you define it to be,* anything and everything your heart desires, anything and

19

everything that is in alignment with your true purpose in life.

These ten principles and practices are the heart and soul of this book. I'll list them now; we'll explore each of them in more depth later:

1 • Imagine your ideal scene; focus on the kind of life you want to create for yourself.

2 • Discover your purpose or mission in life, and write it down as simply and clearly as possible.

3 • Create long-term goals, which very well may encompass a lifetime plan, and read them out loud often, preceded with the phrase, *"In an easy and relaxed manner, in a healthy and positive way, in its own perfect time."*

4 • Create short-term goals that support and move you toward your long-term goals.

5 • Visualize your success, and keep the visualization strong by renewing it often.

6 • Learn how to confront and deal with uncomfortable emotions and any other problems that may prevent you from being successful. Master the core belief process.

7 • Become more aware of the voice of your intuition, and the ever-changing range of your emotions.

8 • Learn the art of effective communication; master the argument-settling technique.

9 • Do what is in alignment with your ideal scene and purpose in life. Do not compromise; do what is for your greater good and the greater good of others and the planet as a whole.

10 • Realize that your life is perfect, just as it is, here and now.

    Most of these principles are easy to grasp—it is *practicing* them that may be difficult. I invite you, I encourage you, to work with this book, to use it as a tool, and to develop your own 'personal power kit' that you use *daily* to create the life you want.

    The rewards are certainly worth the effort.

2

Creating
The Perfect Life
Mentally

———————— • ————————

*Mind is the master power that molds
  and makes,
And we are Mind, and evermore we take
The tool of thought, and shaping what
  we will,
Bring forth a thousand joys, a thousand ills.
We think in secret, and it comes to pass —
Our environment is but our looking glass.*

—James Allen
As You Think

L̲et's begin with a simple exercise. Take a moment to go through it, and you will gain something valuable.

AN EXERCISE

Sit comfortably, relax your arms, relax your hands in your lap, close your eyes. Take three slow, deep breaths; as you exhale slowly the first time, relax your body; as you exhale slowly the second time, relax your mind; as you exhale slowly the third time, let everything go, let yourself feel completely, totally relaxed.

Enjoy the feeling for a moment, breathing softly. It feels so good to consciously relax.

Now ask your intuitive mind to absorb, easily and effortlessly, any and all information that is necessary for you, in this book and in your life in general, to create the life you want. There is something valuable here for you, at this moment, and you intuitively know what it is. Repeat to yourself, *"I am now, easily and effortlessly, absorbing all the information I need. . . . I am now, easily and effortlessly, learning how to create the life I want. . . . I am now, easily and effortlessly, creating the perfect life for me."*

Take a few more deep breaths, and notice how good those words feel to you (feel free to change the words if better ones come to mind). You are ready. Take one last deep breath and open your eyes, feeling refreshed and relaxed, ready, willing, and able to change your life for the better, in any way you desire.

This exercise is very effective before any kind of study, any time you want to absorb information. As with all forms of instruction to your subconscious mind—whether spoken instructions, or some form of meditation or deep hypnosis—use words that resonate positively and powerfully for you. Feel free to change any of these words and make them appropriate for you. Each one of us is a unique individual; each one of us intuitively knows what words are most effective for us.

The exercise will open you up, intuitively, to a greater degree than you were before. Even if it has no other noticeable effect than to help you relax for a minute or two, it is certainly worthwhile.

UNDERSTANDING MENTALLY

Worthwhile learning has three distinct stages:

1 • We have to read or hear the information; in order to truly do this, we have to be open and receptive.

2 • We have to personally relate to and assimilate the information so that we understand it, and see its truth in our own experience. *In this stage, information becomes knowledge.*

3 • Finally, we have to *live* this knowledge fully, embody it, and practice it every moment of our lives. *In this stage, knowledge becomes wisdom.*

Many people make the mistake of thinking that because they understand something intellectually, they are living it in their lives. Yet their lives still leave so much to be desired—physically, emotionally, mentally, and spiritually. They have only heard words in their heads; the words have not penetrated to their hearts, or their subconscious minds; the words have not affected their life experience. *Information has not become knowledge; knowledge has not become wisdom.*

It is important to recognize the difference between thinking you know something, and living that knowledge. It is important to be honest with yourself, at every moment, and to be honest with others. It is important to know whether you're merely repeating information you have heard, or whether that information has become knowledge, and has had an impact on the quality of your life.

Understanding mentally is an essential first step—yet it is only the beginning in creating the life we want. *Everything we have created in our lives was first a thought, and then a feeling, before it manifested as something tangible.*

We are all creative beings, creating everything we have in our lives, at every moment, for better or worse. Some people use their creative energy for success, some for failure; some create works of art, some destroy what others create; some create a mansion on a hill, some create a bottle of cheap wine in the wino district. Each is a creative act.

To create the kind of life we truly want, we first have to make a clear mental map of where we want to go, a map that is in alignment with our greatest purpose in life, a map that excites us, and resonates with our feelings. Then we have to deal with any negative feelings or personal problems that may prevent us from following that map, and reaching those goals. We will know we have dealt with those feelings and problems successfully when we have attained our goals, and created in reality the life we want.

YOUR 'IDEAL SCENE'

One of the most important keys to attaining success is knowing that success is whatever *you* define it to be. You have the ability to create the life *you* want—the perfect life for you—the life that embodies your deepest dreams and fantasies, and your highest aspirations. This is not necessarily the life your parents want for you, or the life you think you should have because it is safe, secure, and sensible.

Take some time to assess what *you* want to create in your life. It will be time well spent. Take time to dream, to fantasize, and to eventually develop a plan, a mental map, that will lead you where you want to go.

The most effective way I have found to begin creating a clear mental map is to do the 'ideal scene' process. I *highly* recommend that you write it down, and place it in a folder or notebook of some kind. This is the first element of your 'personal power kit.' The ideal scene process is simple and fun—and an important first step.

STEP 1
Imagine
your
ideal
scene.

• **Imagine your ideal scene; focus on the kind of life you want to create for yourself.** Imagine five years have passed. In those five years everything has happened to you in the best possible way you can imagine; you have created your success in an easy and relaxed manner, in a healthy and positive way.

What will you be doing, ideally? What have you accomplished? What does a typical day in your life look like? Where will you be living? What will your home look like? What will your relationships be like? What would you be doing to contribute to a better world?

Feel free to let your imagination go. Let it be as farfetched as possible. Shoot for the moon! Let it be *ideal*—we'll deal with reality later.

Be sure to write it down. Don't worry that the writing will make it too concrete—your ideal scene is not carved in stone; you can always change it later, if you wish. Just play with it, have fun with it.

Take a sheet of paper and write "MY IDEAL SCENE" at the top. Then let your imagination soar.

YOUR PURPOSE IN LIFE

Re-read and reflect upon your ideal scene. Imagine

as vividly as you can that you are actually living it; take a moment to enjoy how it feels. This kind of fantasy is healthy and lucrative, for within your ideal scene is a great deal of information about you—information that can lead to knowledge and wisdom. Your 'ideal scene' contains many of your long-term goals—and it also contains, if you reflect upon it, your purpose or mission in life.

This is your next important step.

STEP 2
Discover
your
purpose
or mission
in life.

• **Discover your purpose or mission in life, and write it down as simply and clearly as possible.** Every one of us has a purpose or mission in life. It is up to each of us to define it, to focus on it, and to reach for it. Take another sheet of paper and put "MY PURPOSE IN LIFE" at the top. Then write it, in one short, concise paragraph.

Your true purpose or mission is much broader than any particular long-term goal, and you will want to state it in the highest, most expansive form you can imagine. Though your purpose or mission in life is very broad, it can be stated in a few words. It is also very personal—it is yours alone. Put it in your folder or notebook with your ideal scene, and you have taken another step toward becoming a powerful person able to manifest your dreams. Powerful people know their purpose, their mission, in life.

James Allen, in his great book *As You Think*, written nearly a century ago, reflects beautifully upon this:

Until thought is linked with purpose there is no intelligent accomplishment. With most people, the bark of their thinking is allowed to drift upon the ocean of life. Aimlessness is a vice, and such drifting must not continue for those who would steer clear of catastrophe and destruction.

Those who have no central purpose in their lives fall an easy prey to petty worries, fears, troubles, and self-pitying, all of which are indications of weakness, and which lead, just as surely as deliberately planned crimes (though by a different route), to failure, unhappiness, and loss, for weakness cannot persist in a power-evolving universe.

We need to conceive of a legitimate purpose in our heart, and set out to accomplish it. We should make this purpose the centralizing point of our thoughts. It may take the form of a spiritual ideal, or it may be a material object, according to our nature at the time; but whichever it is, we should steadily focus our thought-forces upon the object which we have set before ourselves. We should make this purpose our supreme duty, and devote ourselves to its attainment, not allowing our thoughts to wander away into ephemeral fancies, longings, and imaginings. This is the royal road to self-control and true concentration of thought.

> Even if we fail again and again to accomplish our purpose—as we necessarily must until our weakness is overcome—the *strength of character gained* will be the measure of our *true* success, and this will form a new starting point for future power and triumph.[1]

Write your purpose down. It is an important element in the notebook or folder you are creating, your 'personal power kit'—the most valuable folder you have. I keep mine in the top drawer of my desk, a manila folder with these words written on the front, in large letters, "I am now creating the life I want." And I have signed it with my name and affirmed it with my heart.

LONG-TERM GOALS

We have taken the time to create our 'ideal scene,' we have reflected upon our purpose or mission in life, and we have put it on paper. Now we're ready for another part of our power package: making a list of long-term goals.

STEP 3
Create
long-
term
goals.

• **Create long-term goals, which very well may encompass a lifetime plan. Read them out loud often to keep them in mind.** The most effective long-term goals have five qualities:

1 • *Your goals must be measurable.* "I am successful" is not the best way to phrase that goal; it is far too vague. What does success mean to you in measurable terms? "I have an annual income of over

$100,000"—that is an example of a measurable goal; you either attain it or you don't, and there is no question about it in your mind. Another possibility might be, "I work twenty hours a week or less, pay all my expenses easily and effortlessly, and save fifteen percent of my income for my retirement fund." Again, find your own words for your own goals.

2 • *You alone are responsible for the achievement of your goals.* "Total world peace," for instance, is a fine goal, but it is not easily achieved by one individual. Contributing to world peace through some measurable activity, however, is an excellent goal. Your goals should be dependent upon you alone to reach them.

3 • *Your goals must arise out of your own desire and be emotionally exciting for you.* Too many people want to become something or have something because their parents or spouses want them to; too many people don't dare leave the security of a large organization and plunge into an activity or a lifestyle that really excites them. The key to true, lasting fulfillment is to create the life *you* want, not the life someone else wants you to have—and not even the life you think you *should* have. What do you really want? If you could be, do, or have anything, what would it be?

If the words "billionaire rock star" leap to mind, for example, that is certainly a challenging goal. Even if you don't fully achieve it, the life you create by reaching for it will be fulfilling for you—*if* that goal also meets the last two important conditions:

4 • *Your goals must be in alignment with your ideal scene and your purpose in life.* If your goals are not aligned with your ideals and purpose, you are working against yourself. An important key to personal power, to creating what you want in life, is to focus upon what is important for you, and eliminate as much unnecessary distraction as possible in your daily life.

Powerful people don't waste time on frivolous activities—anything that distracts you and moves you in a direction other than straight ahead toward your highest long-term goals and purpose in life. Of course, we all need rest, relaxation, and recreation—these are not frivolous; they're essential for our well-being.

5 • *Your goals should in no way harm others.* This includes humans, animals, and the environment. If what you do harms others, the effects of your actions will eventually return to haunt you, and you will never achieve happiness and fulfillment. As you sow, so you shall reap.

What is the difference between long-term and short-term goals? I consider my goals long-term if they take over six months to accomplish, and I have developed my own system to clearly mark the difference: My long-term goals are kept in the folder in my top desk drawer; my short-term goals are entered into my daily calendar notebook that I carry around with me.

I recommend two more things to complete the main part of your personal power kit:
Take a sheet of paper, and type or print at the top:

IN AN EASY AND RELAXED MANNER,
IN A HEALTHY AND POSITIVE WAY,
IN ITS OWN PERFECT TIME. . .

Then list every important, worthwhile long-term goal you can think of. Begin with your most immediate long-term goals, then list others that may require many months or years to accomplish. Include your goal for a specific amount of income. You may want to end your list with this phrase: "I live my ideal scene," and then put your ideal scene in writing.
At the bottom, centered in full caps, add the words:

SO BE IT—SO IT IS.

You may or may not choose to include this. I like it because it is strong and concrete. I highlight the phrases at the top and bottom with a yellow highlight marker.
Read your list, preferably out loud, at least once a day for at least twenty-one days, saying the

phrase, *"In an easy and relaxed manner, in a healthy and positive way, in its own perfect time. . ."* before each of your goals. After the three-week period, say your goals as often as necessary to continue to keep them implanted in your mind.

When you have attained a goal, congratulate yourself, and cross it off your list. Periodically re-write or retype the list to keep it clean and current, preferably every six months, perhaps on New Year's Day and then again in mid-summer.

You will find this exercise to be very effective, for the following reasons:

1 • It keeps you focused on your goals; it keeps them in the forefront of your consciousness. This puts your powerfully creative subconscious to work and moves you toward your goals far more quickly.

2 • It helps you expand and become a more powerful person simply by repeating the goals to yourself. It helps dissolve doubts and fears and other emotional blocks; it reinforces the fact that you are a powerful, creative person.

3 • Repetition of the phrase, *"In an easy and relaxed manner, in a healthy and positive way. . ."* before every goal has a great side effect: After doing the exercise for several days the words sink deeply into your subconscious mind. Before you know it, without conscious effort, events in your daily life that would have been stressful in the past become re-solved in an easy and relaxed manner. When a

stressful situation arises, these words will automatically come to mind, relaxing you and opening up your mind to all the opportunities that are present in every adversity. And you will find a solution in an easy and relaxed manner, in a healthy and positive way, in its own perfect time.

Some people have difficulty with the phrase, *"in its own perfect time."* Effective goals, as we have seen, should be measurable, and one way to measure them is to set a specific deadline. If you have a goal of creating a specific annual income, for example, and then precede those words with "in its own perfect time," isn't this a contradiction?

It *is* a contradiction to your rational mind, but it doesn't seem to be something that bothers you on a subconscious level. If you don't reach your goal within a given time period, the phrase, "in its own perfect time" is an excellent reminder that things are unfolding in their own time, a time schedule often beyond us. Even though it is valuable to make specific deadlines, it is just as important not to become frustrated or, worse yet, defeated if those goals aren't reached as quickly as you would like.

As Rilke wrote in *Letters to a Young Poet*, with regard to accomplishing something important, *"ten years is nothing."* I often think of that when I am focusing on my goals in life. We live in a frenetic, work-oriented culture; many of us feel that looking even five years ahead is an impossibly long time. A year may seem like a long, long time away. Yet a year flies by so quickly—and if we are floating aimlessly through life, we have accomplished nothing more to move us significantly toward our long-term goals. Make definite dates for your long-term goals whenever possible. But don't feel defeated if you have to revise those dates, again and again if necessary. The goals will be met in their own perfect time—and ten years is nothing, in the grander scheme of time, your subconscious mind, and events in the world.

Your personal power kit is nearly complete; it has all the essential elements: your ideal scene, your purpose in life, and your list of long-term goals.

I have a few other things in my folder that you may or may not want to add:

- The most recent pages of my journal. If you're a journal writer, this is a good place to keep it—near your long-range goals.
- A summary of the steps of the 'core belief process,' which we'll get to in the next chapter.
- Various notes to myself and inspiring quotes from others I want to keep and remember. The most inspiring quote I came across recently, for example, is *"Act as if it were impossible to fail"* (from *Wake Up and Live* by Dorothea Brande). I keep these quotes in my notebook and review them from time to time for fun and inspiration. Act as if it were impossible to fail! If you did so, how would you act? What would you do?

SHORT-TERM GOALS

Every long-term goal can be broken down into a series of short-term goals, which leads us to:

STEP 4
Create
short-
term
goals.

• **Create short-term goals that support and move you toward your long-term goals.** When you reflect upon any long-term goal, the short-term steps—at least the first ones—become obvious. I have a long-term goal, for example, of finishing this book and getting it successfully published (and by "successfully," I have written down a specific number of copies sold in the first year, and in the first five years). The first short-term goal that comes to mind is for me to schedule the time several mornings a week to write the first rough draft. Once I finish the rough draft, the next step will become obvious: either re-write the book myself, or get an editor to assist me.

When I set up my long-range goal of creating a successful publishing company, I had no idea of all the short-term steps necessary to reach that goal. But the first short-term goals seemed obvious: Get a job, save some money, then use that money to publish my first book. Once I had reached those short-term goals, the next series of short-term goals became obvious. By keeping the long-range goal of a *successful* publishing company in mind, I was led to discover how to create a successful business.

My goal as I write it on my sheet of paper isn't just, "I have a successful publishing company." It is more specific and measurable: "I have a publishing company with sales of over $_____ and pretax profits of over $_____. I personally make a salary of $_____, plus royalties of at least $_____, and a year-end bonus of $_____ totalling over $_____ annual income from the company."

I make that same goal, every year, with different numbers for the year. It's fun to make goals that specific—and even more fun to reach them, and revise them for the next year with larger numbers.

Every long-term goal can be broken down into a series of short-term goals. Developing short-term goals is an ever-changing, ongoing process that involves playing with every possibility that comes to mind, then sitting down and making a list of priorities.

Here's the most effective tool I have found for achieving short-term goals, in an easy and relaxed manner, in a healthy and positive way. I have developed my own system, which I keep modifying— you will probably want to modify it too, to fit your own style of working.

Use a simple, good quality three-ring notebook as your short-term goal organizer, or any commercial calendar or organizer. Some have room to write your goals, and other things as well. These can be used effectively, but you may prefer to make your own, with the following elements:

- The first twelve pages are a monthly calendar, with the current month on top. You should be able to see the current month at a glance, all major appointments, events, and deadlines you have set for yourself for the accomplishment of short-term goals.
- The next thirty-one pages are a daily calendar, with a page for a day. Stationery stores sell sets of pages with tabs from one to thirty-one, so you can quickly locate any particular day of the month. Type up a page that works for you, and make copies that you can three-hole punch to put in your notebook. Other daily pages are available commercially. You might include a schedule for the day, and spaces for the day's objectives, calls you need to make, and tax-deductible expenses you have incurred throughout the day.

   If you don't do something you have listed under "objectives" or "calls," transfer it to the next day. Write in your expenses and try to remember to staple the receipts onto the page. Then at the end of the year, you will have complete documentation of your expenses for tax purposes.

   I have used this system for many years, and recently have simplified it by buying a desk-top calendar with a week on a page and using it in conjunction with the notebook. My life has become simpler, and I don't need a full page for a day.
- Behind the daily calendar, put in another series of pages with tabs that are alphabetical rather than numerical. These can also be purchased in an office

supply store, and using them will keep you organized and help you to track a wide variety of activities.

In this alphabetical section, make notes to yourself about the ongoing development of all your projects that constitute your short- and even long-term goals. When you have meetings and phone calls, jot down notes, brief minutes of everything that is important to remember. Over months and years with this system, you will have a detailed diary of every step taken in every project. This will help to keep your projects moving ahead and refresh your memory about what has happened in the past.

Be sure to date every entry, of course. Make notes to yourself in this notebook rather than on scattered little pieces of paper. One of the best things about this system is that it does not rely on memory for important details: Every significant detail is jotted down. Many times I have made an agreement with someone, only to find later on that we have different versions of exactly what that agreement was. In these cases, I open my notebook and find the notes that describe our agreement, and when we made it. This has proven invaluable, as our memories are often faulty, especially when recalling specific spoken agreements that were made years before.

- The final element in your notebook is an additional page of paper in the pocket of the inside cover. Here you can keep a list of any ongoing projects or

DAY OF _____

OBJECTIVES	SCHEDULE
	9 AM
	9:30
	10
	10:30
	11
	11:30
	12 PM
	12:30
	1
	1:30
	2
	2:30
	3
CALL	3:30
	4
	4:30
	5
	5:30
EXPENSES	6
	6:30
	7
	7:30
	8

possibilities that don't necessarily fit into the system—notes to yourself, things you want to remember. Review this list often, and take action on whatever you can.

YOUR PERSONAL POWER KIT

Once your notebook is put together and you are using it daily (or nearly so), the elements of your 'personal power kit' are all in place: You have your folder with your long-term goals and other items that we have discussed, and you have your three-ring binder or notebook to keep you organized and assist you in accomplishing your short-term goals easily and effortlessly.

In order to use your three-ring binder most effectively, think of it as the conduit between your long-range goals and your daily life. Whatever form of notebook you develop, it should be something that allows you to take those long-range goals that you are affirming to yourself and break those goals down into short-term steps that you can clearly map out in your notebook.

If you have a long-range goal of creating your own successful business, for example, you could start with a page headed "Business Plan" in your notebook. This is where you will brainstorm every possibility that comes to mind, and eventually develop a full-fledged, workable business plan. The first step or two can be clearly mapped out in the calendar within your notebook. That step may simply be "Talk to Uncle Harry," or "Go to the library and check out a basic business textbook." Whatever it is, schedule it into your calendar on a specific date. Take that first small step, and the next small step will soon become obvious.

Don't worry if you find yourself rescheduling often, moving something you had planned to do today to tomorrow or next week. You may have scheduled things too optimistically, miscalculating how long a trip to the library, for example, or a visit to Uncle Harry would really take. If you don't complete everything on today's list, that's fine— just reschedule what you didn't get done. Keep moving at your own pace. Do something nearly every day, and you'll be surprised at the progress you have made toward a major goal over a period of months.

THE MYSTICAL SIDE

This system of creating long-term goals and breaking them down into short-term goals has a mystical side that is worth reflecting upon: *A subtle but powerfully creative process is set in motion when a long-range goal is supported by focused short-term activities.*

On the surface, it may seem obvious: We create long-term goals on paper, repeat them so we will remember them, and then break them down into short-term goals. Of course this will help us achieve our goals. But it is not as simple as it seems, for if it were a great many more people would be doing it and creating success for themselves. Actually doing the process requires a certain amount of intelligence and discipline—enough intelligence to grasp the concept and enough discipline to review your goals for at least twenty-one days and then on a regular basis after that. It also requires enough discipline to work with your notebook nearly daily to stay focused on your short-term goals.

Once you start to do this process, you will discover that you have begun to release a mysterious energy by focusing specifically upon your goals. The first indication of the workings of the mystical side of this process is usually the number of "coincidences" that start happening to move you toward your goal in ways you could not have foreseen.

In my experience, many examples of this have occurred. I noticed a while ago, for example, that sales of one of the first books I had written had steadily declined, until we were selling very few copies each year. I re-read much of the book, and felt it was still beneficial to others and still worth putting some energy into it in some way.

I asked my intuitive mind to guide me. Should I try to get some radio interviews? Should I create a flyer for bookstores or advertise in some magazines? Should I do some seminars based on the material? I asked what I should do, then waited for an answer. I didn't at the time receive any clear intuitive guidance as to what I should do. The only thing I decided was to make a short-term goal to put some kind of energy into the book.

Shortly afterwards, I was contacted by a German publishing company that was interested in reprinting the book in Germany, and this led to a Dutch translation as well. Soon after that, a major radio station called and wanted to interview me about the book. Sales began to pick up—was this merely a coincidence?

I had a strong feeling, as I have had so often before, that these things probably would not have happened if I had not decided to put some energy into the book. In this case I did very little, almost nothing, except to *decide* to support the book in some way. It is difficult to prove, but something I sense is true, because it has happened so often. The reason is mysterious but very real:

As soon as you commit yourself to a goal that is in alignment with your purpose in life, and as soon as you take a concrete step toward the achievement of that goal, you have created an energy that has an impact upon the world, causing other things to happen, externally, beyond your conscious control, that assist you in moving toward that goal.

We are evolving beings, and by moving forward, consciously, in our evolution, we subconsciously summon the power of nature, the power of the universe, to assist us. It is not necessary to know *why* this miracle works. All that we need to know is that by daring to stretch out and reach for our highest goals and purpose in life, we will receive the support we need.

The great German writer Goethe summed it up in two famous lines of poetry:

> *Whatever you can do, or dream you can, begin it.*
> *Boldness has genius, power, and magic in it.*

Genius, power, and magic: all three come from sources beyond our conscious mind. And all three can be summoned, by imagining our highest goals and taking a small step, even if that step seems tentative, fearful, or childish.

Even small steps are powerful. They affirm to our creative subconscious mind that we have created a mental map of what we want in life, and are willing to take whatever action is necessary to move ourselves toward it.

VISUALIZE YOUR SUCCESS

You have already created, mentally and on paper, a clear picture of the life you want, at this moment in time, and you have begun to take the first steps in that direction. Now you're ready for the next step:

STEP 5
Visualize
your
success.

48

• **Visualize your success and keep the visualization strong by renewing it often.** Every one of your long-term goals will culminate in success of some kind, success you have defined clearly and specifically. The last long-term goal you will want to create is your ideal scene.

As you repeat these goals to yourself, and think about them often, visualize yourself attaining your goals, and keep the visualization strong by renewing it often. With nearly every goal you create—for reasons we will see in the next chapter—there may be a tendency to have doubts and fears, mental and emotional resistance to improving the quality of your life. Your doubts and fears combine to form powerful negative images that can only be overcome through powerful positive visualization.

You will never succeed in any endeavor in which your fears and doubts outweigh your belief in your ability to succeed. "You will become as great as your dominant aspiration," is the way James Allen put it. If your dominant aspiration is clouded with fear and doubt, you will realize those fears and doubts instead of success.

You create whatever you dwell upon and visualize, no more, no less.

As you focus on each of your goals, *feel* yourself attaining it. Eventually, your life will change dramatically enough so that every time you look around at the home and work environment you have created, you will visualize success, for you will see it right before your eyes.

You have taken the first important steps toward creating the life you want—the perfect life for you. You have created a clear mental map, and are moving step by step, goal by goal, toward it. You are visualizing your success, and keeping the visualization fresh in your mind.

Now take another important step and create what you want *emotionally*. This means that you will want to focus not only on the positive, exciting emotions that surround and empower the things you want in life, but also means dealing with all the so-called negative emotions, beliefs, and problems that may prevent you from getting what you want in life in an easy and relaxed manner, in a healthy and positive way.

3

Creating
The Perfect Life
Emotionally

———————— • ————————

*Only by much searching and mining are
gold and diamonds obtained, and you can
find every truth connected with your being,
if you will dig deep into the mine of your
soul. The fact that you are the maker of
your character, the molder of your life,
and the builder of your destiny, you may
unerringly prove, if you will watch, control, and alter your thoughts, tracing their
effects upon yourself, upon others, and
upon your life and circumstances, linking
cause and effect by patient practice and
investigation, and utilizing your every
experience—even the most trivial, every-
day occurrence—as a means of obtaining
that knowledge of yourself which leads to
understanding, wisdom, and power.*

—James Allen
<u>As You Think</u>

The title of this chapter has two important meanings:

The first is that it is not only possible but highly desirable to create a life experience for ourselves that is emotionally satisfying. We don't need to be under constant stress at work, or frustrated at home. We don't need to be adversely affected by our frenetic, workaholic society. We don't need to be trapped in addictive behavior. We don't need to feel pressured about money, or resentful about past or present relationships. It is much more satisfying to be happy, fulfilled, content, and even *serene*. These are worthwhile goals—and this book gives you the tools to achieve these goals.

Creating a life that is satisfying emotionally doesn't mean to deny, to try to transcend, or to "re-program" so-called negative emotions. Every one of our emotions is valuable, important, and necessary, and none should be denied. But it is certainly valuable to create a goal of a life that is emotionally satisfying, and to work toward that goal.

Secondly, in order to fully create the kind of life we want, we need to repeatedly focus on our emotional states, and make sure we are not preventing ourselves from achieving our goals. As we saw in the last chapter, we can easily envision the kind of life we want mentally. It's fun to imagine a five-year ideal scene; it's fun to create goals and affirm that we are reaching them in an easy and relaxed manner, in a healthy and positive way.

As soon as we create any worthwhile goal, however, we are challenging ourselves to expand, to grow, to explore new territory. As soon as we do this, we encounter our own emotional resistance, and we reach what is for most people the most important step on the ladder to fulfillment:

STEP 6 Learn to confront and deal with emotions.

• **Learn how to confront and deal with uncomfortable emotions and any other problems that may prevent you from being successful; master the core belief process.** Before we can reach our goals and create a perfect life, our emotional resistance must be effectively dealt with. This is important to understand, so important that it must become an ongoing awareness—*knowledge* that we apply constantly in our daily lives. As we explore our emotional resistance in depth, we take our knowledge to heart, and it becomes wisdom—the true emotional understanding that gives us the power to create the perfect life.

EMOTIONAL RESISTANCE

We have created goals that feel wonderful, goals that are aligned with our highest purpose in life, goals that expand us and move us much closer to true and deep fulfillment in our lives. We are affirming to ourselves daily that we are achieving these goals in an easy and relaxed manner, in a healthy and positive way.

Yet with many of these goals, we encounter emotional resistance, in many different forms:

seemingly endless varieties of fears, skepticism, doubts, anxiety, disbelief, self-criticism, excuses, procrastination, and self-defeating habits. We encounter inner voices that tell us *we don't deserve to be successful*; we don't have the ability, the talent, the connections, the money, the luck, or whatever it may take to create the life we want.

Why do we have this emotional resistance in the first place? Why do we resist our own success? Within the many answers to this question is the knowledge, and ultimately the wisdom, that can help us effectively overcome our emotional resistance.

Before you read further, ask yourself this question, and try to answer it as honestly as possible: Why do I resist creating what I want in life? It is not a simple question; consider the following possible explanations, and see if one or more of them resonates with truth for you:

As soon as we create a worthwhile goal, we are challenging ourselves to expand, to explore new territory—and *new territory can be frightening*. We are forcing ourselves to be creative, demanding that we grow and change and do things in new ways. This brings up a great deal of emotional resistance in nearly everyone.

Every goal also involves taking a risk, and *taking risks is frightening*. Every risk we take, after all, has the possibility of failure—and almost all of us have a fear of failure. Failure can mean poverty; failure can mean ridicule from people that we respect; failure can mean our worst fears are realized.

Making new goals means changing in some way, and this upsets our old, comfortable habits. The power of old habits is a very strong force that works against us as we try to change our lives for the better. Even if we're extremely frustrated with our current situation, at least it is familiar to us, and we are, subconsciously at least, comfortable with it.

As Hamlet said, we would "rather bear those ills we have, than fly to others that we know not of."

Many of us also fear success. We are at least subconsciously aware that success will bring with it a great many new and challenging problems. As Mark Twain said, once you become successful, so many of your former friends find reasons to resent you.

Finally, and perhaps most important, is this: New goals that are based on our dreams and ideals confront all of the negative conditioning we have learned over the course of our lives.

Drs. Hal Stone and Sidra Winkelman clearly describe in their book, *Embracing Our Selves,* how each of us is composed of a large number of subpersonalities. These subpersonalities are often in conflict with each other. Each of us has a creative child within us, and a vulnerable child, and an inner critic. We also have a "pusher," driving us to do more and more, a "protector/controller" trying to maintain order and the status quo, and a great many other subpersonalities. Some are dominant, while others are repressed and disowned.

Each subpersonality has a great number of beliefs about itself—some positive, some negative. Each of us senses on some level, for instance, that we really are creative and have something important to contribute to the world—but we may also have come to believe that we're really not that creative, we can't make much difference in the world, and it's hardly worth the effort to try to make a positive contribution to society. We all have a creative child within us—a creative genius, actually—but too often it is thwarted by a cynical inner critic who has seen it all and knows it doesn't make any difference anyway, so why bother?

We pick up a great deal of negative conditioning over the course of our lives, and we develop a number of deep beliefs, or "core" beliefs, that are very effective at preventing us from creating what we want in life. It is difficult for most of us to confront and grapple with these deep-seated beliefs. We have been working with a very powerful process over the years, called the "core belief process." It has been written about before (in *The Creative Visualization Workbook* by Shakti Gawain), yet this information is essential and worth repeating, until it becomes common knowledge and, better yet, common wisdom.

AN OPEN ATTITUDE

It is not necessary, incidentally, to *believe* that these ideas or exercises will work for you. You only have to dare to try something new, and experiment a bit. Try the exercise that follows—the "core belief process"—with an open mind, and see what happens for you. Don't accept what I say or what anyone else says as truth, until you have tested it in the laboratory of your personal experience. Then form your own conclusions; the information you gather from others has to become your own knowledge.

These ideas and techniques have evolved from my personal experience and those of a close circle of friends. The foundation of this book is built upon the constant application of these ideas and techniques in my own life. They have worked for me, bringing me a life I could barely dare to dream about several years ago. I have also witnessed the results they have brought to the lives of many others.

These principles and practices will work for anyone who applies them consistently in their life. All that is needed is an open mind. Open yourself up to the possibility that you and your world can be quite different from what you may currently believe. Go ahead—entertain different possibilities; open up to the idea of change. It may be scary at times, but it is time for a change, individually and globally. Look at it as an adventure, a great experiment—one that will improve your life and the world we live in as well.

I encourage you to take the time to work and play with the following material. Take your time, read thoughtfully, and go through the steps of the core belief process. Take the time to question and challenge this material, and question and challenge yourself. It is time well spent.

CLEARING PSYCHOLOGICAL BLOCKS

Every one of us has a number of "psychological blocks" that affect some aspect of our attitudes or behavior. These blocks are based on various fears that we have developed during our lives—usually quite early in life. We experience these fears each time we hold ourselves back, or fail to grow and develop as much as we can or to enjoy our lives as fully as we can. These blocks are obstacles that prevent us from realizing our greatest potential in life, because they prevent us from taking risks, trying new things, and making positive changes in our lives.

Doubts, worries, hesitations, and fears inhibit us, creating a lack of self-esteem and an overly critical attitude toward ourselves or others. Much of what we consider "normal" behavior really stems from a fearful emotional state: Worried parents, frustrated kids, and highly stressful work environments are often accepted as "normal," or even inevitable, yet these situations can be changed.

There is no universal law that says parents have to worry, kids have to be frustrated and rebellious, and work environments have to be stressful.

These emotional states can be changed; the challenge is to take an honest look at them, and discover how to move beyond them. The process is not difficult, but it does require willingness to change, to let go of old, familiar habit patterns, and it takes a certain degree of persistence to establish new and healthier habit patterns.

If you haven't created the kind of life you want, if you haven't attained the level of success you desire, you can be sure you have some psychological blocks to examine, overcome, and let go of. It can be done.

ACCEPTANCE

The first step in this process is often overlooked, but so necessary: The first step is *to completely accept yourself.* If you can fully accept yourself as you are right now, you'll find it much easier to change for the better. *It is all right to have negative feelings,* and you have a lot of company—the entire human race, in fact. Actually, so-called negative feelings serve a useful function: They keep us discontent, so we are forced to examine ourselves, which is necessary in order to improve our situation, to grow and develop, and to eventually become stronger, clearer, wiser—and able to fulfill our greatest potential in life.

Accept yourself, as you are now, in this moment. Ask yourself if there are things about yourself that you are not accepting, things you feel frustrated, guilty, angry, or fearful about. Take an honest look at each of these feelings, one at a time, and then embrace each one as being, for the present, an acceptable part of you. *Embrace all of your selves*, every part of your being. All these things have been necessary for your development so far. Accept them, and you will find it much easier to either live with them or let them go.

Accept your friends and family, as they are, too. Accept your boss and co-workers; accept everyone you come in contact with, even those you dislike or disagree with. Every one of us is doing the best we can. Acceptance doesn't mean that you have to put up with anything you don't feel good about, or that you can't express your honest feelings to others. Quite the contrary—once you thoroughly accept yourself and others, you'll find it much easier to give honest feedback, and this feedback is more effective, more readily heard. (We'll deal with this more fully in Chapter Four.)

CORE BELIEFS

Next we have to discover the *cause* of our emotional blocks. Why do we resist change, and success? What is at the root of our psychological blocks? Once we find the cause, we have taken a giant step toward the cure. A great many psychologists, teachers, therapists, scientists, religious leaders, philosophers, intellectuals, writers, and others have tried to answer this question. A great many theories have been enumerated, including heredity, environment, our parents or dysfunctional family, disease, codependence, genetic coding, cultural heritage, physical defects, mental defects, misplaced sexual energy, disowned selves, emotional instability, sins we have committed, evil in the world, our lack of understanding, ignorance of the laws of karma, and a myriad of other reasons that a great many creative, and sometimes desperate, imaginations have devised.

Most of these theories blame factors beyond our control, and that makes it difficult, if not impossible, to change our behavior. How can we change our early environment, which is now a thing of the past, or a dysfunctional family? It is certainly impossible to change our heredity, genetic coding, or our parents.

We must not only find the causes of our psychological blocks, *we need to understand these causes in such a way that enables us to do something about them.* Now consider the following theory. Live with it and work with it a while, and see if you find it useful for you: *The causes of our psychological blocks are the particular "core beliefs" that we have formed about ourselves, other people, or our world.* A "core belief" is an idea or attitude that we *accept as truth*, either consciously or unconsciously.

This is a crucially important concept, one that bears repeating until we fully grasp all of its ramifications. For once we understand and work with this concept, we discover the power to change our lives for the better.

In our earliest childhood, we learn to accept certain things as either true or false in our world. Many of these things were oft-repeated words from Mommy or Daddy: We are good little kids, or bad kids; bright or stupid, or sloppy, or silly, or pretty, or goofy-looking, or dirty, or talented, or lazy, or hyperactive, and so forth. Many of these ideas were things our brothers, sisters, and peers told us, and often we accepted them, unconsciously.

Our experience in the school system usually adds a great many negative core beliefs as well, with highly competitive sports, grading systems, and even such widely accepted (and questionable) practices as IQ tests. From a very early age, we begin to develop some deep feelings of inadequacy. Very few students come out of the school system with a positive self-image, daring to dream of the greatest success imaginable. Very few students leave school feeling like a winner, yet we can *all* become winners—each in our own way—once we understand the power of our core beliefs and thought processes.

Many of these beliefs are harmful and negative; many are contradictory, and cause confusion. Here are some typical examples of negative core beliefs:

I'm inadequate; I'm not complete in some way; I need someone else or something else to be happy; I'll never succeed; it's impossible to make enough money these days; I don't know how to manage money—if I had it I'd probably just blow it anyway; the world is a dangerous place; my parents didn't raise me right; I had a deprived childhood; love is dangerous—I might get hurt, or hurt someone; deep down, I can't *really* love anyone; I don't really have any close friends; I'm not okay; there's something wrong with me; I'm unworthy and undeserving; people (including me) are basically bad—selfish, cruel, stupid, untrustworthy, sinful; there's not enough (love, money, good things) to go around, so I have to struggle to get my share; creating success in my life would mean eighty-hour work weeks or other things I'm not capable of; it's hopeless, I'll never get enough; if I have a lot, someone else will have to do without; money is the root of all evil; money corrupts; the rich get richer and the poor get poorer; the world doesn't work and never will—in fact, it's getting worse all the time.[2]

As you read through these negative beliefs, see whether any of them reflect an underlying assumption of your own belief system. If so, you've taken the first step toward changing that belief, for *once you have consciously identified a core belief, you can begin to consciously change it.* For core beliefs aren't necessarily true or false in themselves, only our thinking makes it so.

Every one of us who is not succeeding at something has a great many reasons for justifying our lack of success—and our reasons are valid, because they are obviously true for us in the present.

Now, take a moment to reflect upon this: It doesn't matter what has happened to you in the past—what matters *now* are the particular dominant core beliefs you accept and carry around with you, because these beliefs influence your behavior and your basic experience of life.

Core beliefs are self-fulfilling prophesies. If you believe you can't sing, for example, you certainly can't do it. If you try to sing, you will only work against yourself, and ultimately fail. This failure in turn becomes another reason to support your initial core belief that you really can't sing at all. Every day we see the confirmation of our beliefs. In fact, the world and everyone in it seems to act in accordance with our beliefs.

CHANGING YOUR CORE BELIEFS

How can we change our core beliefs? It's quite simple, surprisingly simple for those of us who think any process of change has to be difficult, complex, mysterious, or painful. First, you have to accurately identify the core belief, in the simplest possible words. Then you gradually discard it by repeatedly affirming, with emotional conviction, a new belief that contradicts the old one and works better for you.

Repeat this process as often and as many times as necessary until your negative core belief changes for the better. You'll know the core belief has changed when your experiences change and you begin to see definite improvements in your life.

The next time you catch yourself saying or thinking that it's hard to make enough money doing what you want for a living, or you find yourself dwelling on what you don't have or affirming that you *can't* have what you want, drop the word *can't* from your vocabulary and tell yourself you *can* have what you want. Tell yourself repeatedly, until you are thoroughly convinced, mentally and emotionally. The "core belief process" that follows will show you step-by-step how to do this effectively.

AN EXAMPLE OF THE CORE BELIEF PROCESS

Before we go through the steps of the core belief process, I'd like to give you an example of how I used this process to deal with a problem I faced several years ago. This particular example is still vivid in my mind and I still use the affirmation I came up with quite often.

One day I received a notice from a credit card company, informing me in computerese that I was over my limit and needed to send six hundred dollars immediately, over and above my regular payment. This was not good news, since I didn't have six hundred dollars available—in fact, I had very little money at all. I got in my car and headed for my travel agent to pick up some expensive airline tickets for a trip I had booked only a few days before the flight. I realized that I could have saved hundreds of dollars if I hadn't procrastinated so long before buying my tickets. Of course, I was paying for the flight the same way I would have to pay off the six hundred dollars: with yet another credit card.

I felt agitated and frustrated. I knew that behind my frustration, some core belief was lurking that needed to be examined. I went through the steps of the core belief process, talking out loud to myself in the car:

I asked myself, *what is the problem?* I answered, the problem is that I am still frustrated with the issue of *money*. I feel out of control financially. I feel stupid. I'm not managing my personal finances nearly as well as I manage my business. It doesn't seem to matter *how* much I make because I simply spend more and more. Even though I've been achieving my goals for my personal income, I have no control over my spending habits.

Then I asked, *what emotions am I feeling?* I'm feeling frustration; I'm angry and agitated. There's fear underneath it all.

What physical sensations am I feeling? I have an agitated feeling in my stomach, almost a panicky sensation. I have tension in my neck and shoulders, and in my face. I'm uptight!

What am I thinking about it all? I'm thinking that I'm really stupid. I'm blaming myself for being out of control. I've been borrowing on credit cards for years as if it weren't really money at all, and now I'm at least thirty thousand dollars in debt. That's really *dumb*. I'm paying five thousand a year in interest alone! How did I get into this mess? I've been spending more than I make for years. I barely have any savings, in spite of an income that puts me in the top five percent of the country. I feel like an idiot!

What is the worst thing that could happen? The bottom will completely drop out of my life. I'll suddenly find myself with my back against the wall, with no means to pay my massive debt, and have to declare bankruptcy.

What would be the worst thing that could happen after that? I'd lose my business, I'd lose my home—everything. I'd be out on the street, homeless and begging for quarters.

What would be the very worst thing that could possibly happen? I'd commit suicide or die of disease—cold, in pain, alone, abandoned on the streets. (I know this sounds melodramatic, but these were the thoughts that went through my mind, and it's very valuable to explore these extreme fears.)

Now, what is the best *thing that could possibly happen?* I get completely in control of my life financially. I consistently earn more money than I spend. I create a quantum leap in my income, so that all my debt is nothing; I pay it off effortlessly. I easily and effortlessly create my ideal scene, forever abundant, with several million dollars in liquid assets. I only use credit cards for convenience, and pay them off in full every month.

What fears or negative beliefs are keeping me from creating what I want? I fear that I am out of control; I am not sensible. I believe that I am not really capable of creating financial success.

What affirmation can counteract and correct those fears and beliefs? These words sprang to mind immediately: *"I am sensible and in control of my finances at all times. I am building total financial success."*

I said this statement over and over, until I knew it could be true, until I felt that it was possible to achieve. Emotionally, the words felt wonderful. As soon as I parked my car, I wrote the words down on the back of a business card. Eventually, I wrote the affirmation on four different cards, and put one in my billfold and the others on my desk at home, on my desk at work, and on my dresser in my bedroom. I kept those words in front of me and repeated them often.

Soon I began to feel in control of things; I felt as if I had a handle on the money problem. I still had no specific plan, nothing concrete, but the affirmation showed me that a solution was possible.

Gradually, over a period of several months, the solution appeared to me. It was, like most effective solutions, a very simple one. It enabled me to both increase my income and reduce my debt. Most importantly, however, I was able to dramatically decrease the amount of anxiety I felt around the issue of money.

I had taken a good look at the core belief that was causing me frustration and resentment and limiting what I wanted to do in life. And I found a way to change that belief. Each day of my life, I experience the proof that this belief has changed. Today, I am sensible and in control of my finances; I am building total financial success.

You, too, are capable of being sensible and in control of your finances. You, too, are capable of building total financial success. Learning to use the core belief process can help you to achieve your highest goals in life—whatever they may be.

THE CORE BELIEF PROCESS

At times, it can be a challenge to discover a core belief and express it in a simple, brief sentence that gets to the heart of the problem we're creating for ourselves. Core beliefs can be elusive, especially for those of us who tend to intellectualize a great deal— the "rampant rational mind" type—or for those who tend to become engulfed in overwhelming emotions—the "rampant emotional" type. While there is certainly nothing wrong with either our rational minds or our emotions, the two need to be balanced, and in harmony. When one begins to dominate the other, we lose touch with our natural, innate clarity, and create far more problems for ourselves than necessary.

Whenever we are feeling emotionally upset, it can seem especially difficult to identify the core belief that is operating. The core belief process is designed to identify these beliefs in the midst of an emotional problem, or following an emotional event that remains unresolved.

The process can be done by yourself or with a partner. If done with a partner, one of you should ask the questions while the other answers, taking just a few minutes for each question. If you do it alone, you can write down your answers to each question, answer them silently or out loud to yourself, or speak into a tape recorder and replay the tape afterward.

To begin, sit silently for a moment. Take a deep breath, and relax as you exhale. Then think of the particular situation, problem, or area of your life that you want to improve.

Now proceed through the following steps:

1 • **Describe the nature of the problem, situation, or area of your life you want to work on.** Take about three or four minutes to talk about it in general.

2 • **What emotions are you feeling?** Name the specific emotion, such as fear, sadness, anger, guilt. Do not

describe any particular thoughts you are having about it at this point.

3 • **What physical sensations are you feeling?**

4 • **What are you thinking about it?** What conditioning or "programming" can you identify? What negative thoughts, fears, or worries are you having? Take a few minutes to describe your thoughts.

5 • **What is the worst thing that could happen in this situation? What is your greatest fear?** If that happened, then what would be the worst thing that could happen? What if that happened? Then what would be the *very* worst thing that could possibly happen?

6 • **What is the best thing that could possibly happen?** Describe the way you would ideally like it to be, your "ideal scene" in this area of your life.

7 • **What fear or negative belief is keeping you from creating what you want in this situation?** Once you have explored this question, write your negative belief in one sentence, as simply and precisely as you can. If you have more than one, write down each of them.

8 • **Create an affirmation to counteract and correct the negative belief.** There will be more about affirmations in the next section, but for now, here are some guidelines:

   • The affirmation should be short, as simple as possible, and meaningful to you. For example: "I am a worthy person. I deserve to be successful!"

- It should be in the present tense, as if it is already happening. For example: "I now have abundance in my life."
- The affirmation should be the opposite of your negative core belief. Turn the negative thought into a positive, expansive one. Some examples follow:

Negative belief: "I don't have enough time to do the things I want to do."

Affirmation: "I have plenty of time to do the things I want to do."

Negative belief: "The world is a dangerous place."

Affirmation: "I now live in a safe, wonderful world."

Negative belief: "I have to struggle to survive."

Affirmation: "I am creating total success in an easy and relaxed manner, in a healthy and positive way."

Negative belief: "I'm under a lot of stress at work; it's unavoidable in my high-pressure job."

Affirmation: "I now relax and enjoy myself at work, and accomplish everything easily and successfully."

Negative belief: "Money corrupts people."

Affirmation: "The more money that comes into my life, the more power I have to do good for myself, for others, and for the world."

- Your affirmation should feel exactly right for you, and cause a strong, positive emotional feeling. If it doesn't feel right, keep changing it until it does.

9 • **Say or write your affirmation repeatedly:**
- Repeat your affirmation silently to yourself, while relaxing. Picture everything working out exactly as you want it to.
- Write your affirmation ten or twenty times a day, until you feel you have absorbed it as a positive core belief. If negative thoughts arise as you write your affirmations, write your negative thoughts on the back of the paper, then keep writing the affirmation on the front until it feels free of any emotional resistance.[3]

That's the entire core belief process. Feel free to play with it and modify it to suit your own particular needs. I've seen it have a profound and positive effect on a great many people, including myself. All you need is a willingness to be honest with yourself. Your spontaneous answers to these questions may surprise you. After completing the process, most people experience a wave of relief, something that can be described as feeling a lot *lighter*. It's as if we had been carrying around an emotional weight on our shoulders, one we weren't even fully aware of, and we have suddenly let it go. The result can be exhilarating.

THE POWER OF AFFIRMATIONS
AND VISUALIZATION

As you do the core belief process, you discover that the right affirmations can have a deep and positive effect on you. In fact, they can change your life. *Affirmations are the single most powerful tool we have for creating the life we want, for they can literally change our negative core beliefs into positive ones.*

There is nothing difficult or esoteric about doing affirmations; it is a natural process we are doing all the time, sometimes consciously, but more often unconsciously.

The word affirmation comes from the Latin word *affirmare*, which literally means "to make firm." Affirmations do indeed "make firm," literally creating the reality we desire. How can this be?

We are naturally creative beings. In the broadest, deepest sense, we have all created our present life situation. We create our own experience of reality, although most often, we do it subconsciously. We create the life situations that we feel, in some way, we deserve. The core beliefs we accept about ourselves lead us subconsciously to create the life we're living.

How do we create something? How do we write a book or knit a sweater? How do we repair a leaky sink or fill a living room with furniture? First, we develop an intention to do something; that is, we *affirm* to ourselves that we're going to do it. "I'm going to write a book. . . . I think I'll knit a sweater. . . . I've got to repair that leaky faucet. . . . We need some new living room furniture. . . ." All of these are affirmations, words that "make firm" your intention to do something.

Once the intention is firm, we summon the creative power of our mind and visualize the results. We do this so often that the process is usually automatic. Both our conscious, linear, verbal mind and our subconscious, intuitive, spontaneous mind have the power to visualize results. When visualization is done repeatedly, and when it is supported by our mental and physical energy, we create what we are affirming and visualizing.

Note that the word "visualizing" does not necessarily mean literally "seeing" the final results in actual form in our "mind's eye," though this is sometimes what happens. Visualizing is often done in a nonvisual form; it can be described as a know-ingness or a certainty. When you say, for example, "I'm going to the store for some milk and cookies," this simple statement involves both an affirmation and a visualization: You "see" yourself going to the store, in some way—you imagine the possibility of going to the store—and you affirm that you will do so by your statement, whether it's spoken out loud or just a thought in your mind. Your affirmation and visualization direct your body to move in a certain direction, and you create your desired reality—in this case, milk and cookies.

We are constantly visualizing and affirming, but too often we do it unconsciously, and in a way that creates negative results. Many of our words and thoughts reflect core beliefs we developed at an early age: I can't do this; I'm incapable; this is too hard for me to handle; I don't know how; I'm unattractive; and so on. Our core beliefs are also a result of the barrage of negativity from the media and from other people: The world is a mess; it's so hard to succeed in today's world; taxes are too high; it's so hard to find the right person; I need something else to make me happy; I need to do something to make me more attractive; and so on.

It's unfortunate, but these ideas—whether spoken out loud or hardly noticed inner dialogue—are powerful affirmations that will create the reality we are affirming.

Fortunately, it is not that difficult to overcome even a lifetime of negative self-conditioning; all it takes is the desire to change, an understanding of the process, and perseverance. When you find yourself thinking negative thoughts, or saying negative things, replace those old words with new, positive words. Start seeing yourself as strong and capable, surrounded by a great many fine possibilities—infinite possibilities! As you create positive, supportive core beliefs to replace the old, worn-out ones, you will find your life becoming much more enjoyable. You will be surprised at how quickly positive results appear in your life.

As Richard Bach has written, "Argue for your limitations and they are yours." How true! Focus on your strengths instead, and they will become even stronger. Focus on your dreams, and they will become your reality.

James Allen has written, in the hundred-year-old classic *As You Think*:

> *You will become as great as your dominant aspiration. . . . If you cherish a vision, a lofty ideal in your heart, you will realize it.*

As I write this, that quote is on my wall in front of me, in large, bold letters. It is a constant reminder, a powerful, self-fulfilling affirmation: *"I cherish a vision, a lofty ideal in my heart, and I am now realizing it."* How much better to let words like these guide our lives, rather than words of limitation. You can do whatever you want in life—all you need is the key that will unlock your own "vision and lofty ideals." That key is your power to affirm and visualize, a power you have always had.

AN EXERCISE IN VISUALIZATION AND AFFIRMATION

I highly recommend the following short exercise. It requires only a few minutes each day, four or five days a week, in order to create positive results in just a few weeks.

During these few minutes, relax, suspend all your critical, rational, or "realistic" beliefs, and *visualize* your ideal scene, *affirming* that you already have it. This simple exercise can be used to create *anything* you desire: health, wealth, wisdom, happiness, serenity, a relationship, a peaceful environment, a new car, a good grade on a test, the solution to a problem, or whatever you may want.

> Sit, or lie down comfortably. Close your eyes. Take a few deep breaths, and relax thoroughly. . . relax your body. . . relax your mind. . . let everything go—all worry, all thought, all doubts. . . . As you relax, enjoy the feeling of simply breathing, simply relaxing.
>
> Now picture, as clearly and in as detailed a manner as you can, whatever you want to create. Imagine your ideal scene as clearly as you can, as if you have already created it, and are enjoying it. Picture as many details as possible. Spend a minute or two focusing on this, enjoying the imaginary scene you are creating.
>
> Then, find affirmations that nourish and support your visualization, and repeat them to yourself, over and over. An example might be something like, *"I am now in perfect health,"* or *"I have now received a promotion, which has increased my salary to _____ dollars per year."*
>
> A more expansive affirmation could be *"I now have a beautiful home in the country that I pay for easily and effortlessly, with lots of land,*

views of nature, and a large quiet studio where I create works of art that bring me over $200,000 a year in income, easily and effortlessly. So be it—so it is!"

Take a moment to enjoy and savor whatever "fantasy" you have created. Add a few more details, and play with your visualization, until it feels as if it already exists in the world.

Finish by taking one more deep, relaxing breath and affirm to yourself, *"This, or something better, is now manifesting for the highest good of all concerned. So be it—so it is!"* (You may want to put this very important final thought in your own words.)

Open your eyes and come back to the present moment, feeling refreshed and relaxed, feeling the happiness and contentment that comes with achieving what your heart desires.

Repeat this exercise, focusing on the same thing, at least four or five times a week, preferably every day. Soon—within two or three weeks—you will have absorbed your visualization deeply into your subconscious mind, and will begin to see concrete results in your life. You will find yourself moving inexorably toward the manifestation of your vision.

In the last example, we're visualizing goals that will probably take years to reach, yet we should still feel some concrete results quite quickly. The first small, achievable steps will emerge: perhaps you'll start a new creative project, or have a brainstorm and realize how to make more money, or decide to take a course in real estate—there are infinite possibilities. As you continue to visualize your ideal scene, you will be led, step by step, to its fulfillment.

Remember, *you will become as great as your dominant aspiration. . . . If you cherish a vision, a lofty ideal in your heart, you will realize it.*

If the desired results don't begin to appear in a reasonable amount of time, chances are you're blocking yourself in some way. Go back to the core belief process and find out what core beliefs may be preventing you from getting what you want, and *deserve*, in your life.

If you are regularly visualizing, doing the core belief process, taking appropriate steps toward your goal, and *still* not getting what you want, you may be trying for too much too soon. Make your short-term goals—those things you can expect to accomplish in about six months or less—realistic. Total world peace, for example, is not a realistic short-term goal at the present time. But the peaceful solution to specific problems may be. Building a mansion in the country and creating a successful career as an artist with a high seven-figure salary may also be too ambitious for short-term goals, but looking for and finding a specific way to increase your income by a specific amount that feels achievable is an excellent short-term goal.

Make your long-term goals, on the other hand, as idealistic and expansive as you want. This inspires you to stretch further toward your greatest potential. Your ideal scene *is* an achievable long-term goal. You can develop all the long-term goals you wish, then break them down into achievable, short-term steps. Take one step at a time up the ladder, using visualization, affirmation, and, when necessary, the core belief process. Before too long, you will be at the top.

This technique of conscious visualization and affirmation is very simple, it is true, and may seem too simple to those who feel that it should be more complex in order to be effective. But after using the process for a while, you will become much more aware of what you are thinking and what you are picturing for yourself *every moment throughout the day*, even in your dreams. By taking the time to imagine and affirm what you want in your life, and by becoming aware of what you are picturing in your mind and affirming to yourself every moment, you open the gates to the boundless power of your creative imagination. I have found this to be true in my own experience, and I challenge you to try a similar experiment on yourself.

WATCH WHAT YOU SAY!

When you do these exercises, you will naturally become much more aware of every word you say—

and you'll eventually even become aware of every negative thought that drifts through your mind. So many of the habitual phrases we repeat to ourselves or to others have a power to limit us and prevent us from creating the life we want. As you do this process, you'll become aware of all these phrases—and as you weed them out of your speech and thought, your life will improve dramatically.

So many people constantly repeat negative thoughts and words, and then wonder why their lives are still a mess: "This job is killing me. . . that makes me sick. . . oh, my aching back. . . I *hate* this. . ." and so on. These words send powerful messages to your subconscious mind. Swear words, too, wreak subconscious havoc. Watch what you say; words have a great deal of power, both for good and for ill.

As Margaret Atwood wrote, *A word after a word after a word is power.*

OVERCOMING FEAR OF FAILURE

Those of you who are courageous enough to actually *do* the core belief process—and it does take courage—will discover a common denominator to all of the core beliefs that do not support you in getting what you want in life: *fear.* More specifically, *fear of failure.*

Remember the personal example I gave of the core belief process? Underneath my anxiety was the fear of total economic failure. That fear dissolved, gradually, over the years, as I continued to work with the core belief process and continued to affirm *I am sensible and in control of my finances; I am building total financial success, easily and effortlessly.*

Has my fear of economic failure been *totally* dissolved? Probably not, but it doesn't create much anxiety in my life anymore. I still have some fear of economic failure at times, and it serves a valuable purpose: it keeps me from taking risks that aren't sensible, or becoming over-leveraged, or too greedy. Far too many people have lost millions—even billions—of dollars, and have gone from riches to rags. You can fail financially regardless of your level of income or assets. It is one of my goals and affirmations to keep my wealth building, in an easy and relaxed manner, in a healthy and positive way.

Every successful person I have ever heard of has experienced failure before they became successful. Failure serves a valuable purpose: *it creates the foundation for success.* Failure is far more educational than success, because we learn more with every failure than we do with success. I've certainly had my share of failures, yet every failure I have had has contributed to my success. I consider my failures to be the cost of my education—and education is necessary and ongoing.

I heard a profound bit of conversation quoted from the old *Amos 'n' Andy* television show. Amos (or Andy, I forget which) says to Kingfish,

"Kingfish, where did you get your good judgment?"

"From my experience."

"And where did you get your experience?"

"From bad judgment."

Failure, and the bad judgment that precedes it, are necessary ingredients in creating success. *It's okay to fail*—everyone who tries something new has done it, repeatedly. Look at a child beginning to walk. Every one of us who learns to walk has had our share of falls and bumps and bruises.

Someone once used this analogy about failure: A pilot flying a plane is off course ninety-nine percent of the time. But the pilot just keeps correcting, and correcting, over and over. When we go off course, we sometimes fail—but our failures teach us more than our successes. Success happens when you are physically, mentally, emotionally, and spiritually aligned. Every failure shows you that, in some way, you're out of alignment. So then you correct yourself, and get back on course.

The only real failure is in quitting. As long as what you do is in alignment with your highest purpose in life, you need not fear failure, for you will be guided step by step toward reaching your goals. The experience you gain from your failures, miscalculations, and poor judgment will inevitably lead you to success. There is one exception, however: If you waste your time and resources through addictive behavior, it is difficult, if not impossible, to truly succeed.

DEALING WITH ADDICTIONS

I picked up a hitchhiker once who was pleasant-looking, humorous, obviously intelligent. He said his car had recently been repossessed and, as we talked further, he said he had lost his job, his wife, his children, and his home because of his addiction to gambling at race tracks. He wasn't sure what he was going to do next; he had no idea as to how to put his life back together—and he was on his way to the race track, once again.

All of us have seen how addictive behavior can prevent someone from getting what he or she wants in life. Each of us has to honestly assess our lifestyle and habits and determine whether addictive behavior is keeping us from achieving our goals and purpose in life. All the techniques for attaining success in the world will never work if you undermine yourself through addictive, self-destructive behavior.

Fortunately, there are plenty of choices we have to remedy the situation. The principles upon which Alcoholics Anonymous are founded are brilliant, and have proven wonderfully effective in resolving the problems created by addictive behavior. These principles can be applied to virtually every kind of addiction anyone has experienced.

There are many other organizations and other philosophies, of course, that effectively deal with addictions as well. We all have access to them, and we should feel no hesitation in using their resources, if necessary. Some of the most brilliant and successful people in the world, after all, have had to wrestle with addictions, and were not afraid to ask for help.

EMOTIONS AS INTUITIVE GUIDANCE

The techniques given in this chapter and the following chapter—especially the core belief process and the argument-settling technique—help us deal with our emotions, especially the so-called "negative" emotions, in a healthy, constructive way.

Now we can focus on what is, for most of us, the most exciting arena of our emotional experience: *emotions are the gateway to our intuitive guidance.*

This is the next step in our life's journey:

STEP 7 Become aware of your intuition.

• **Become more aware of the voice of your intuition, and the ever-changing range of your emotions.** Every emotion we feel—whether "good" or "bad," joy, anger, contentment, depression, enthusiasm, fear, ecstasy, boredom, love, hate, fascination, revulsion—has a very important reason for being. Every emotion opens us up to our vast intuitive resources, and offers us the guidance we need in any moment. The more aware we are of our ever-changing range of emotions, the more intuitive information we receive.

We all have "gut feelings," intuitive hunches. To some degree, we are all able to tune into a vast amount of intuitive information about ourselves, about others, and about our world. Solutions to our problems become apparent, not through an elaborate process of rational thought, but through an instantaneous gut-level knowingness of the best thing to do.

Watch a child, especially a newborn or an infant; watch the way emotions dance across a baby's face. They change constantly, from radiant love to curiosity, to fear, to rage—all in a few seconds. Each of us still has that emotional child within us; it is a vitally important aspect of our personality. The more we become aware of how we feel, in every moment, the more easily we can make decisions that are necessary to create the kind of success we want in life.

How are you feeling right now? Take a moment to answer this question. The more you ask yourself that question, the more you become aware of the ever-changing range of your emotions.

When you are fully aware of your feelings, you can also *act* in a way that supports your emotional experience. So many of us take actions throughout the day that violate us emotionally. We work in a stressful job we don't like, for example, or spend time with friends or relatives who are unsupportive or undermine our confidence in some way.

We need to support ourselves, and our friends and business associates, as much as we possibly can in doing what is in harmony with our ever-changing range of emotions. This is a difficult challenge—but a deeply rewarding one. By being totally honest with ourselves, and willing to act upon our feelings, we are guided, moment by moment, to truly create the perfect life.

4

The Art of
Effective
Communication

———————— • ————————

*As a being of power, intelligence, and
love, and the lord of your own thoughts,
you hold the key to every situation, and
contain within yourself that transforming
and regenerative agency by which you
may make yourself what you will.*

—James Allen
<u>As You Think</u>

4 • *The Art of Effective Communication*

Success is built upon relationships; no one can create success in a vacuum. Even a writer who works alone all day needs an agent, a publisher, or some contact with the outside world to produce and market his or her work. If you define success as living as a complete hermit in the woods, avoiding all contact with humanity, you may be the exception to the rule. But in general, successful people need a network of relationships with others to reach their goals.

An important ingredient in creating the kind of life we want is to have satisfying, healthy, honest, and open relationships with those around us. There may be people, it is true, who have attained what appears to be success and yet have stressful, bitter relationships with the people they live and work with. But who really wants or needs the stress of frustrating relationships? What good does it serve?

It is sad but true that most of us have worked for people or have known people who have done quite well in attaining financial success but have been miserable failures at creating satisfying personal and professional relationships with those around them. They simply have not been taught and don't understand a vitally important key to successful relationships: effective communication.

EFFECTIVE COMMUNICATION

This is an essential step in our growth, an essential part of our inevitable success:

STEP 8
Learn
how to
communicate.

• **Learn the art of effective communication; master the argument-settling technique.** Communication is an art, and can be learned like any other art. Unfortunately, most of us have not been taught to communicate effectively, especially when we're angry, upset, worried, or depressed. It is hard to express irritation with others so that they understand us and do not become upset and reject everything we say. Many people don't believe it's possible, and don't even try to talk about their feelings until their irritation develops into an overwhelming anger that bursts out uncontrollably and causes more anger, hurt, and guilt.

This is unfortunate, because if we take the time to learn how to talk to each other in a way that minimizes alienation, we will come closer together, understand each other more deeply, and discover a new kind of love and appreciation, rather than drifting apart.

In any kind of relationship—whether with employers or co-workers, professional associates, families, friends, lovers, neighbors, or international relations between countries—*everyone involved has the right, and must be given the opportunity, to speak their minds freely.* If the relationship is to work successfully, everyone must have their say; otherwise, destructive feelings can develop. Ultimately, hostile feelings and separation (even war!) are the result of a breakdown in communication.

One of the most valuable things we can ever learn is how to communicate our honest feelings and offer our honest feedback without making people feel that they've been attacked, or inundated with built-up resentment, anger, and criticism.

There is a specific technique for this. It works best when you find yourself in the middle of an argument. The technique can also be modified and used in ordinary conversation. For many of us, the next section may be one of the most important sections in this book.

THE ARGUMENT-SETTLING TECHNIQUE

One of the most interesting things about this technique is that you can use it whether the other person is willing to go through the steps with you or not. To explain it clearly, however, I'll assume that both parties are aware of the technique and willing to use it. Once you understand how it works, you can easily modify it to use with an unwilling partner. After all, you both win in the end, and that's the best part of successful communication.

When you find yourself locked into an argument with someone, or when you have something to say that has been bothering you, go through these steps:

1 • **Stop arguing**. Once you become locked into an argument, you are getting nowhere. Both of you are trying so hard to be heard that neither one is listening; neither of you is open to hearing what the

other wants to say. Arguing compounds the problem, rather than solving it—so just make the decision to stop arguing and abide by the rules of the game. Remember, it takes two to tangle; if you refuse to argue, your opponent can't continue the argument for long.

2 • **Allow your partner to completely express his or her feelings,** without interruption, and without denying what they are saying, defending yourself, or putting yourself or anyone else down.

Simply listen to, and accept, what your partner is saying. This is the most challenging step, since it is especially difficult not to interrupt or react negatively. But it is also the most important step, because it allows your partner to express his or her feelings without interruption. It also teaches you to absorb criticism without immediately reacting verbally—and this is an *extremely* valuable skill to gain.

When you first go through this process you will probably find it very difficult—almost agonizing—not to interrupt. But it is *essential* that you learn to listen without interrupting. If your partner is especially angry, if difficulties between you have built up for a long period of time, he or she may be throwing many different feelings and issues at you that you want to respond to immediately. It can be difficult to remember everything that's coming at you; when I first did this process, I had a notebook at hand, and made brief notes of what was said so I could remember to respond to every point. It's all right to take notes, as long as you keep listening and *don't interrupt*. Your partner will finish what he or she has to say, usually in a surprisingly short amount of time— though it may not *feel* like a short amount of time.

3 • **Now it's your turn to express your feelings, as completely as possible,** and your partner must be quiet and listen. Encourage your partner to hear what you're saying without denial or defense, or without putting anyone down in any way. If your partner interrupts, remind him or her that you listened without interrupting, and you want them to do the same for you. Your partner will get another turn in a few minutes.

Take as much time as you need. In my experience with this technique, it usually takes less than five minutes for each person to "blow off their steam" and express everything there is to say.

After the second person has finished, the first person usually wants to respond, and at this point, the second and third steps may be repeated as many times as necessary (very rarely is it necessary to repeat them more than two or three times). Before long, you'll find the air clearing between you. You'll realize how the constant interruptions of your earlier arguments kept fueling those arguments. When you stop interrupting each other and listen instead, the heat of the argument vanishes.

Now you can move on to the next step:

4 • **Ask your partner what he or she wants from you,** providing the time and encouragement, without

interruption, for your partner to tell you exactly what he or she wants and needs. Listen and remember. Every argument is based on the fact that the people involved aren't getting something they want. Then:

5 • **Tell your partner exactly what you want from him or her.** Now you're ready for the final step:

6 • **Negotiate with each other.** Make clear agreements that work for both of you. Compromise may be necessary for one or both of you, but keep negotiating until you reach an agreement you can both be satisfied with: a "win-win" agreement. It may require some time and creative brainstorming to come to agreement, but in almost every case you can find a creative solution that works for *both* of you.

WHY THE ARGUMENT-SETTLING TECHNIQUE WORKS

Why does this simple technique work so effectively? There are at least three reasons:

1 • When arguments start, we stop listening. Frustration builds, and we say things that only make matters worse. As the argument builds in intensity, covert cutting remarks become overt, negative criticism or just downright stupid, thoughtless remarks. No one likes criticism or anger directed at them. The natural response is self-defense and anger. By using this technique, you get the satisfaction of having expressed your feelings in an environment where those feelings are heard—and frustration dissolves.

2 • You can't get away with the all-too-common reactions of denial, defense, or putting yourself or someone else down. You are forced to listen, accept, and absorb what the other person is saying. In other words, you are forced into a more mature and intelligent response—a *wiser* response, one that teaches you to be more open to other's opinions and feelings, and to grow as an individual. You don't necessarily have to agree with what the other person is saying. You are completely free to disagree with what you hear, if you feel, for any reason, that what they're saying is not appropriate for you. But you must at least be willing to hear what the other person is saying, and take a moment to consider it without an immediate verbal reaction. In a surprisingly short time, this takes the steam out of an argument.

3 • By learning to simply listen to others, without interrupting and without defending yourself, another fascinating thing often happens: You start to *empathize* with other people, to see why they feel what they feel, and to sympathize with them and understand them more fully. You gain insight into the tremendous diversity of human feelings, the wonderful complexity of human relations. You find yourself broadening, gaining much more experience—the experience of another person's perspective. You gain a great deal of knowledge and, eventually, wisdom.

Almost any problem can be solved in such a way that everyone involved wins. It may take quite a bit of negotiation, creative thinking, and compromise; it may involve breaking large problems down into smaller, specific problems; but there is almost always a solution to be found that will work satisfactorily for everyone involved.

Again, once you understand how to use the argument-settling technique, you can use it effectively with people who don't know you're using it. If you find yourself in an argument, simply stop and say, "Look, this argument is getting us nowhere. I'm going to sit here and listen to everything you have to say—*without interrupting you*—and then I'm going to ask you to listen to what I have to say, without interrupting me—okay?" They will almost always agree, because all they really want is to be heard.

Then let them have their say; let them release their pent-up frustration, without denying it or being defensive. Again, *don't interrupt*—sometimes it will seem to be the most difficult thing in the world, but it is *essential* not to interrupt. Wait until they are finished. Then say, "All right—I listened to you. Now I'm asking you to listen to me, and not to interrupt me until I'm finished. Then I'll listen to you again, *without interrupting*—okay?"

In this way, you can take them through every step of the technique, even if they never agreed to go through the process in the first place.

FEEDBACK AND PERSONAL POWER

When you use this technique, you learn another valuable lesson: the importance of the feedback you receive from others. You may notice when you go through the process that your natural tendency when confronted with something you don't like to hear is denial, immediate self-defense, or putting yourself or others down in some way. To simply allow yourself to hear what others are saying, and absorb it and consider it without denying it, may seem very difficult at first.

If we can develop a different attitude about the feedback we receive from others, this "open listening" can become easy, even enjoyable. A more intelligent attitude is this: *Almost everything anyone says to us is useful in some way.* We may not like it, we may not agree with it, we may not accept it as being true, but there is some useful information in almost everything that is said to us.

Once you develop the core belief that you are basically a strong and worthwhile person, someone who has something to contribute to the world, you will find that you naturally feel confident and clear when relating to friends, relatives, lovers, co-workers, everyone. You will find that you can listen to everything they have to say, accept the fact that they are speaking what they believe to be true, and usually discover something worthwhile in what they are saying. Although you may not agree, you can definitely be open to hearing what others have to say.

This is the attitude of a powerful person, a person who is not threatened by others and doesn't have to deny, defend, or apologize.

AGREEMENTS, COMMITMENTS, AND NEGOTIATION

Another reason the argument-settling technique is so effective is that it inevitably leads you into a negotiation process that results in making clear agreements and commitments with the people around you. Agreements and commitments are essential in creating the life you want, yet so many people are afraid of making them. Many people are afraid of the negotiation process in general.

There is nothing to fear in agreements, commitments, and the process of negotiation—as long as the goal is to create a "win-win" situation for everyone involved. The later steps of the argument-settling technique require you to ask what the other person wants from you, and to tell the other person what you want from him or her. This naturally develops into a process of negotiation that in the long run serves everyone.

GETTING INTO ALIGNMENT

Getting into alignment with the people you work and live with is another important aspect of effective communication. Just as the tires on your car need to be in alignment so they won't wear out prematurely, we need to be in alignment with those around us, working toward similar goals, or toward goals that are in harmony with each other. Relationships, and businesses, often run into difficulties because those involved aren't in alignment with each other about specific goals or more general life purposes. The need for agreement seems so obvious, yet how many people working together, and how many people living together, honestly examine the compatibility of their goals, purposes, and dreams? This seldom happens because there is usually no framework within which to do it. To provide such a framework, try playing the following game, another form of the "ideal scene" process:

> Sit down with your companion or business associate—anyone you work with or relate to on a regular basis—and pretend that five years have passed. During those five years, everything went as well as could possibly be expected for everyone involved. You are well on your way to achieving your "ideal scene" in life—the perfect life. In this future, what are you doing? Where are you living? What is your typical day like? What kind of relationship do you have? Each player takes a turn describing this ideal scene. The more detail you can provide, the better.

As we saw when we did this process alone, this simple technique is highly effective in clarifying long-range objectives. It leads us to discover something very important to every one of us: our goals in life, and even our greater *purpose* in life, something we rarely reflect on but feel deep within ourselves, whether we pay any attention to it or not.

Once you have talked through your "ideal scene" together, you can develop long-range plans that will satisfy *all* your needs and dreams, and move each of you toward your particular ideal. This exercise forces you either to come into alignment with each other or to see that it is not possible for you to do so.

It is certainly challenging—but not impossible—to create the life you want when you are living or working with people whose goals contradict yours, or who, for any reason, won't support you in achieving your goals.

One of my favorite quotes—written in large type and displayed on my wall—is from Mark Twain:

> *Keep away from people who try to belittle your ambitions. Small people always do that, but the really great make you feel that you, too, can somehow become great.*

You can become as great as your highest aspirations! These words are undeniably true—when you believe them to be true.

5

The Perfect Life

————————— • —————————

Every night and every morn
Some to misery are born
Every morn and every night
Some are born to sweet delight. . . .
We are led to believe a lie
When we see not through the eye

—T.S. Eliot

These words from T.S. Eliot are powerful and true: "We are led to believe a lie when we see not through the eye."

The eye is the eye of our understanding, knowledge, and wisdom. The lie we are led to believe is the lie of our negative core beliefs: the lie of our doubts and fears; the lie of hopelessness; the lie of failure; the lie that our lives leave so much to be desired; the lie that we're not capable of being successful, powerful, fulfilled, happy, and wise.

The truth is that most of our fears are unfounded, and our negative core beliefs are merely lies and distortions. The truth is that we are fully capable of creating the perfect life—in any way we define that for ourselves. We are capable of being powerful—able to create whatever we want in our lives, able to lead happy and fulfilled lives.

This is true for others, and it is certainly true for you and me. We have all the necessary tools to achieve success in life, in any and every way that we define success.

THE IMPORTANCE OF RELAXATION AND REJUVENATION

We live in a workaholic culture, where the norm is to work all day at our jobs, five days a week, then rush home to deal with the responsibilities of family life. On weekends, we work at home, or shop or do errands. Even going out for pleasure can all too often become another obligation that involves scheduling, traveling, and other kinds of stressful activities. Most people only have a few precious weeks of vacation a year, and often come home from their vacations more exhausted than they were before they left.

Something is missing here, something that is very important to our well-being. Many of us have forgotten, or have never learned, the fine art of relaxation and rejuvenation.

Do you remember as a child, lying flat on your back and watching the clouds go by? Do you remember spending your entire day swimming, skating, hiking, riding your bike, fantasizing, or exploring the neighborhood? Do you remember napping, sleeping on the floor, sleeping wherever you felt like? Children are more in tune with their bodies than most adults—and children know, intuitively, when they need relaxation and rejuvenation.

Most real, effective relaxation and rejuvenation is unstructured and usually spontaneous. If we listen, our bodies will tell us when they want to run, when they want to relax, when they want to eat, and when they want to sleep. I eat only when I'm hungry, sleep when I'm tired, relax when I feel like relaxing, and exercise whenever I feel like it. Most children do this, so why do so many adults create such busy lives that there is no time to do what they want to do—even simple things like taking time to smell the roses, walk in the park, scratch the cat or dog behind the ears, or lie in the yard and stare up at the sky?

Ask yourself what you need to do to relax, rejuvenate, and care for yourself. Each of us is unique; you need to develop your own style of relaxation and rejuvenation.

Meditation is an excellent form of rejuvenation for mind, body, and spirit. In my experience, the simplest forms of Zen meditation have been the most beneficial for me. After spending six months doing Zen meditation, I noticed some definite, very positive changes in my life, physically, mentally, and emotionally. If you are interested in exploring Zen meditation, Philip Kapleau's *Three Pillars of Zen* is a very good guide. There are many forms of meditation in Western traditions also. One of my favorites is the healing meditation described in *The Art of True Healing* by Israel Regardie (see Suggested Reading in the back of this book).

An infinite variety of activities can be relaxing and rejuvenating. I love to take vigorous walks through the hills and run on the beach. I find aerobics classes rejuvenating, energizing, and excellent for stress reduction.

There are also days when I do nothing at all, except read, sleep, eat, and watch TV. I have even tried to be as lazy as my cat—but that's impossible for almost all human beings.

CREATING YOUR IDEAL WORK SCHEDULE

Many people are surprised when they find out what my work schedule is. I have spent a lot of time and thought creating the schedule I want. It seems to me that almost everyone can do this, but so few people try. Why do so many people assume they have to work forty or more hours a week at a job they don't particularly like, or if they are fortunate, at a job they like? Why do so many people assume there is never enough quality time for lovers and family or for their own creative projects? Often we simply assume there aren't enough hours in the day to do everything we need to do *and* have time to relax, rejuvenate ourselves, and even spoil ourselves a bit. Unfortunately, these assumptions, these beliefs, become self-fulfilling prophesies.

Our beliefs are formed in our early years—and we are strongly influenced by our schools and our parents. Children tend to imitate their parents, and most of us are still carrying around a great many core beliefs that are a result of the Great Depression: You have to work really hard to survive, you're lucky if you can get a good job, money doesn't grow on trees, and so on. Our schools, in my opinion, encourage the belief that we must work hard in order to survive in this world. When I was in school, I was far too busy to spend time on my back staring at the clouds, except for those wonderful, long, lazy summer vacations.

Here's the daily scenario that works for me, and I encourage you to develop your own unique scenario. I usually sleep until eight or nine in the morning (I am not a "morning person"), then I get up and exercise with a swim in my pool, a hike through the hills, or an aerobics class. I read the morning paper, with orange juice and a cup of coffee, and then usually spend an hour or two writing or playing music, working on whatever I feel like working on, usually a book or an album project.

I go into the office around one or one-thirty, and work until five or six. Usually I take a lunch break—sometimes a business lunch, sometimes a pleasure lunch. As president and chairman of a successful publishing company, I spend about fifteen hours a week in the office (although I often do work-related reading and writing at home). I could, of course, spend sixty hours a week in the office if I chose to, but I prefer to spend fifteen or twenty at most. My company consists of a staff of fourteen people, and not one of them works a full forty-hour week. In my opinion, a forty-hour work week is inhumane, unless you are so absolutely in love with your work you prefer not to do anything else. Why not do the job more efficiently in fewer hours, get out of the office, and do something else you really want to do?

On Saturdays, I write in the afternoon, do errands, or go out socially. Sundays are almost always wide open, with no plans at all. I want at least one day a week when I can wake up in the morning without one blessed thing to do. Sometimes I do absolutely nothing on Sunday. Other times I accomplish quite a bit, when I feel like doing something on the spur of the moment. If something comes up for a Sunday that I absolutely have to plan on—an important family affair, a staff picnic, a convention—then I keep Saturday or Monday open for relaxation and rejuvenation. At least one day a week is completely unstructured and free.

I always take it easy on Mondays as well, avoiding stressful situations if at all possible. I rarely go into the office or schedule appointments on Mondays. In my opinion, Monday is not the best day to begin a work week—many people feel tired, drained, and emotionally sensitive on Mondays.

How do I maintain this kind of work schedule while running a multimillion dollar business? My schedule is founded on the core belief that I can be successful by working part time. Some of my friends have said they consider me "semi-retired." I disagree, however. I see no need to ever retire, and probably never will. But I believe in working a limited number of hours so that I have time for plenty of other creative activities and leisure activities outside of my regular "job."

Another reason I'm able to have a schedule that is ideal for me is important enough to be a step we should all take. It is something we discussed earlier, and is certainly worth reflecting upon again:

STEP 9
Stay
in
alignment.

• **Do what is in alignment with your ideal scene and purpose in life.** Do not compromise; do what is for your greater good and the greater good of others and the planet as a whole.

The importance of this step is obvious: We reap what we sow, and if we hurt ourselves, others, or our fragile earth in any way, our actions always come back to haunt us, and prevent us from creating what we want in life.

THE MILLIONAIRE CLUB

The focus of this book has been primarily on ourselves—doing the inner work necessary to create our perfect life, first mentally, then emotionally, then finally in physical reality. It can be very helpful to share this process with a sympathetic friend—I stress the word *sympathetic*. If you share your dreams, ideals, and goals with friends or relatives who are not sympathetic, they can do a great deal of damage, weakening your resolve, casting doubts, supporting negative core beliefs. For this reason, I discuss my dreams and goals with very few people, only those I know will support me in the belief that I really can attain my goals.

I have formed a club with a special friend. We call it the "Millionaire Club," and we have put our purpose, guidelines, and goals in writing:

Our purpose is to support and empower each other to create our ideal vision of life.

We have three guidelines:

1 • Meet at least once at the beginning of the month, and communicate throughout the month to keep the visualization of our goals fresh in our minds.

2 • Maintain secrecy. Everything we discuss is confidential.

3 • Maintain a written record of our discussions, goals, and decisions.

This record has become an important part of my 'personal power kit,' and the club has become an exciting and fun part of my life.

Having someone—it can be just one individual, or a small group—who completely supports your dreams and goals definitely helps empower you to reach those goals more easily than if you have to go it alone. Our inner critic is so quick to doubt; having a sympathetic friend can help overcome doubt and negative core beliefs, and create the kind of success we want in life.

SUCCESS

An inspirational thought is displayed on my desk. I have no idea where the words came from, but they have been significant enough in my life that I chose them for the frontispiece of this book:

> *To live your life in your own way*
> *To reach the goals you've set for yourself*
> *To be the person you want to be —*
> *That is success.*

The single most important key to success is this: *Success is whatever* you *define it to be*. You have the inherent ability to create the perfect life for *you*. This does not mean the life your parents want for you, or the life you think you should have because it is safe, secure, reasonable, necessary, or socially proper.

Take time to assess what *you* want in your life. Take time to dream, to fantasize, to go through the process of imagining your ideal scene. If your ideal scene unfolds during the next five years as *fantastically* as you can imagine, what does your life look like? Once you answer this question, you will clearly understand what success means to you. You have all the tools you need to live your life in your own way, to define what success means to you, and to create clear goals for attaining that success.

Once you create the life you truly want, you are in a much better position to help others create better lives, and to do your part in preserving our delicate and sacred planet.

THE PERFECT LIFE

According to the oldest tradition of Tibetan Buddhism, there are nine levels of study; to put it in broader perspective, nine ways to view the world— nine broad levels of consciousness.

The first three are called the *outer* levels, because they involve outwardly changing your appearance and actions, donning robes, becoming a celibate priest, working to serve your community, and so on.

The second three are called the *inner* levels, because they involve inner practices, not outer ones. Various forms of meditation and visualization are examples of inner practices.

The last three are called the *secret* levels—not because anyone attempts to keep them a secret, but because they are so subtle, elusive, and difficult to grasp. The ninth stage, the final stage, is called *dzog chen* ("dzog" rhymes with "vogue") which means "absolute perfection." The practice of *dzog chen* requires no robes, no specific meditation practices —all it requires is understanding the great truth that *our world and our lives are already absolutely perfect, every moment.* This has always been true and will always be true.

This path is an enigmatic one for most of us, because so much of our experience seems to contradict it. What could possibly be perfect about the violence and mass killings by so many governments and individuals throughout the history of our civilization? What is perfect about the devastation of our planet's natural resources?

The perfection in these instances is so hard to grasp that it remains a secret for most people, hidden from view.

The greatest master of the teaching of "absolute perfection" was named Long Chen Pa; he taught in Tibet about seven hundred years ago. His words are the opening quote of the Introduction:

> *Since everything is but an apparition, perfect in being what it is, having nothing to do with good or bad or right or wrong, one might just as well burst out in laughter.*

I adhere to the views of the teachers of "absolute perfection," taught hundreds of years ago in the remote country of Tibet—and still taught today: I believe that our lives are absolutely perfect. I also believe that we can consciously choose to shift our thinking in order to understand this subtle truth.

There is a quote on my desk at the office that tells us how to make this shift: *"For every adversity, there is an equal or greater opportunity."* Problems represent opportunities, in personal life and in business, and yet most people resent their problems, at least on some level. "I don't want to have to deal with this," we may tell ourselves, or "This person is so difficult," or "Why me?" or any number of other responses that do nothing to move us toward a solution.

We can, however, shift our thinking so that we say to ourselves, "I may have this problem, but what is the opportunity for me here? How can this benefit everyone involved?" By looking at it from this perspective, we can turn every adversity into an opportunity.

Every adversity *does* present us with an equal or greater opportunity, if we will only choose to see it that way. Every adversity can also make us stronger, more experienced, and more powerful.

Another way to see the perfection in all things can be summed up in this simple phrase: Everything that happens to us is "a message from the universe."

We are in a constant state of personal growth and evolution. We are always moving toward greater clarity and success, toward more power and wisdom. In a mysterious way, there *is* a message in everything that happens to us—especially those events that we resist or find difficult to accept. The more we look for "the message," the more we become aware of the absolute perfection of our lives and our world—and we see that our lives reflect the image of the ideal scene we hold in our hearts.

There is a large atrium in the center of my home, with no roof. As I write, I can look out at the treetops, green hills, and open sky. A swarm of birds just whipped around the tallest tree in sight and circled it before continuing on their journey. What could be more perfect than this?

My cat lies sleeping on the floor nearby, basking in the warmth of sun through the sliding glass door. What could be more perfect than that?

It is my hope that someday—whether today, tomorrow, next year, or ten years from now—you will look at your life and honestly feel and believe, *"My life is perfect, just as it is, here and now."*

This is the final step:

STEP 10
Your
life is
perfect.

• **Realize that your life is perfect, just as it is, here and now.**

SUMMARY

Let's review the ten steps that are the heart and soul of this book:

1 • Imagine your ideal scene; focus on the kind of life you want to create for yourself.

2 • Discover your purpose or mission in life, and write it down as simply and clearly as possible.

3 • Create long-term goals, which very well may encompass a lifetime plan, and read them out loud often, preceded with the phrase, *"In an easy and relaxed manner, in a healthy and positive way, in its own perfect time."*

4 • Create short-term goals that support and move you toward your long-term goals.

5 • Visualize your success, and keep the visualization strong by renewing it often.

6 • Learn how to confront and deal with uncomfortable emotions and any other problems that may prevent you from being successful. Master the core belief process.

7 • Become more aware of the voice of your intuition, and your ever-changing range of emotions.

8 • Learn the art of effective communication; master the argument-settling technique.

9 • Do what is in alignment with your ideal scene and purpose in life. Do not compromise; do what is for your greater good and the greater good of others and the planet as a whole.

10 • Realize that your life is perfect, just as it is, here and now.

You have within you the power, the ability to create the perfect life for you, in an easy and relaxed manner, in a healthy and positive way, in its own perfect time. You can do it. It is up to you.

Notes

————————————————— • —————————————————

1. James Allen, *As You Think* (New World Library, 1987), pp. 39-40.

2. Many of these core beliefs are reprinted, with permission, from *The Creative Visualization Workbook* by Shakti Gawain (New World Library, 1982).

3. The core belief process was first published in *The Creative Visualization Workbook* (see above), pp. 45-46.

Suggested Reading

———————————— • ————————————

All of the following books, except the last one, are published by New World Library.

As You Think by James Allen, edited and updated by Marc Allen. One of the greatest self-improvement books (or rather, self-*empowerment*) books ever written. It's also available on cassette tape, and I highly recommend repeated listenings.

Creative Visualization by Shakti Gawain. This is destined to become a classic as well. Her writing is simple, clear, and extraordinary.

Living in the Light by Shakti Gawain. This goes beyond *Creative Visualization*, focusing on developing your intuition, though I recommend starting with *Creative Visualization* first.

Embracing Our Selves by Hal Stone, Ph.D. and Sidra Winkelman, Ph.D. The two internationally known therapists who have developed the "Voice Dialogue" method have written the definitive book on subpersonalities. Just reading this book is highly effective therapy. Their work is a very important contribution to the field of psychology. They have also produced a series of excellent cassettes, including "Meeting Your Selves," "The Child Within," "Meet Your Inner Critic," and several others.

Embracing Each Other by Hal Stone, Ph.D. and Sidra Winkelman, Ph.D. A brilliant look at how to make the relationships in your life work.

Work With Passion—How to Do What You Love for a Living by Nancy Anderson. A very helpful book by a master career consultant.

Reflections in the Light by Shakti Gawain. Inspiring daily thoughts and affirmations.

Awakening—A Daily Guide to Conscious Living by Shakti Gawain. Another collection of inspiring daily thoughts and affirmations.

Maps to Ecstasy—Teachings of an Urban Shaman by Gabrielle Roth. An "urban shaman" shows us that we were born to be not simply happy and fulfilled, but even *ecstatic* at times.

Prospering Woman by Ruth Ross, Ph.D. Excellent for men as well as women in enabling us to develop the power we already possess to bring the prosperity we desire into our lives. *"The secret to experiencing joy in life is loving what you have while working toward what you want."*

Anybody Can Write by Jean Bryant. This book gives guidelines not only for writing a journal, but can help you start and finish that book you've been dreaming about.

Letters to a Young Poet by Rainer Maria Rilke. Brilliant advice for each one of us.

Native American Wisdom, edited by Kent Nerburn, Ph.D., and Louise Mengelkoch, M.A. As we read the wisdom of these people, it is impossible not to feel a reconnection with the land, and ultimately, with ourselves.

The Art of True Healing by Israel Regardie. A powerful meditation, effective not only for healing, but for helping us to improve our lives in every possible way.

The Three Pillars of Zen by Roshi P. Kapleau (Doubleday, Anchor Press). A good introduction to Zen meditation, one of the most effective forms for Westerners that I have discovered.

About The Author

———————————•———————————

Marc Allen is co-founder and president of New World Library. He is author of several books, including *Tantra for the West—A Guide to Personal Freedom*. A musician and composer, he has recorded several albums. He lives in Marin County, California, where he divides his time between writing, music, and the publishing company.

New World Library is dedicated to publishing
books and cassettes that help improve the quality
of our lives.

For a catalog of our fine books and cassettes,
contact:

New World Library
58 Paul Drive, San Rafael CA 94903
Phone: (415) 472-2100
FAX: (415) 472-6131

Or call toll free:
(800) 227-3900
In California: (800) 632-2122